Published by
Nima, Dapper
West Sus

GH01464206

Text by Gerald Cole

Illustrations and Cover by Rodney Brown
Centre map by T.O.H. Graphics

Copyright © Firefly Publications 2001

All rights reserved. No part of this publication may be reproduced, stored in a
retrieval system, or transmitted in any form or by any means, electronic, mechanical,
photocopying, recording or otherwise, without either the prior written permission
of the publisher or a licence issued by the Copyright Licensing Agency Ltd,
90 Tottenham Court Road, London W1T 4LP.

ISBN 0 9515691 2 0

Whilst every effort has been made to check the accuracy of the descriptions contained in
this guide, visitors should be aware that opening times, prices and other conditions at
individual sites may change at short notice.

Artwork by Leighton Graphics
Tel: 01329 313440
Typeset in Palatino and Frutiger

Reprographics by MGM Ltd.
Tel: 01273 411221

Printed and bound by D.A.P. Sussex Ltd.
Tel: 01273 430430

GERALD COLE

Author, Gerald Cole, moved to Sussex from Hertfordshire more than a decade ago, living first in the Brighton area before moving to West Sussex. In addition to establishing a reputation as a writer of management books, he has also written and published in the field of local history. He has written about the impact of the Battle of Britain on southern England, and is the author of the companion volume to this one - the Firefly Guide to West Sussex. He feels keenly that people should be aware of, and have a respect for, the history of their locality. His writing aims to describe local history in concise and informative ways. He is a member of the National Trust, English Heritage, Sussex Heritage, the Council for the Protection of Rural England, and the Royal Society for the Protection of Birds. He has been an active member of the Society of Authors for many years.

RODNEY BROWN

Illustrator, Rodney Brown, was born in Cambridgeshire, and educated Kimbolton School, near Huntingdon, where he gained a passion for cricket and athletics under the influence of two giants of those sports - Sir Jack Hobbs and Harold Abrahams. From an early age he was fascinated by drawing and painting. Inspired by his Kimbolton art teacher, Donald Hood-Cree (Slade/Paris), he went on to have his work accepted regularly at the Royal Academy. Rodney moved to Arundel in the early 1960's, and now lives in Angmering. His other interests include the theatre and classical music, where he has exercised his talents locally with the Arundel Players and the Arundel Festival, and nationally with the Royal Philharmonic Orchestra. Today, regular commissions keep him busy at his Angmering studio.

Notes

1. The best maps for finding the places mentioned in this guide are those published by the Ordnance Survey. The most relevant to this guide are the Landranger series (2 cm to 1 km) Nos. 198 & 199, and the Explorer series (4 cm to 1 km) Nos. 122, 123, 124 & 135.
2. There is good road access to all the sites mentioned in the guide, and many are covered by local bus services (see local timetables). Given the rural nature of most of the places described, access by rail is more difficult. However, there are some leaflets for walkers published by the railway companies, indicating walks that may be combined with rail travel.
3. The glossary of terms for visiting churches is designed to help those who are unfamiliar with church architecture and its symbolism.

Cover illustration: features include the Pevensey Gun, Kipling portrait, Fletching Church, former Observatory - Herstmonceux, Bateman's, Bluebell Railway, Fiennes brass - Herstmonceux Church, and Lewes Castle.

A limited number of modestly-priced copies of the illustrations in this Guide may be available on request. If you are interested, please write to the publisher for further details, including your choices.

Firefly Publications, Nima, Dappers Lane, Angmering, West Sussex BN16 4EN   5/01

FIREFLY GUIDE

EAST SUSSEX

History · Culture · Landscape

Contents

Introduction   5

Prehistoric Sites   7

Castles   11

Churches, Abbeys and Priories   17

Stately Homes and Gardens   33

Nature Reserves and Beauty Spots   39

Museums   43

Steam Railways   49

Other Visits   51

Long-distance Paths   53

Glossary for visits to churches   56/57

Map (central spread)   30/31

List of illustrations
Alfriston, Clergy House 34
Battle Abbey 16-17, 19
Beachy Head, Belle Tout Lighthouse 40
Bishopstone, St Andrew's Church 20
Bodiam Castle 12
Brighton Pavilion 32-33, 34
Clayton, Jack and Jill Windmills 52
Eastbourne, Centurion Tank 43, 44
Fletching, St Andrew & St Mary 21
Lewes Priory, Battle of Lewes Monument 24
Lewes, Anne of Cleves House 46
Michelham Priory 25
Pevensey Castle 10-11, 14
Seaford, Martello Tower 48
Wakehurst Place 37
Wilmington, The Long Man 6-7, 9
Winchelsea, Town Seal 28

Introduction

This guide aims to describe some of the outstanding scenery and sights of interest in East Sussex, mainly in rural areas. As a visitor to the county, you will probably want to know something of the history of the places mentioned in this guide. You may also want to understand the countryside environment in which these places are set. On both scores you will almost certainly want to be able to read concise and accurate descriptions of the places you decide to visit. This guide aims to provide just such details, giving historical highlights and locations, as well as opening times, prices and other practical information.

The guide differs from many others in the range of its subject-matter, providing details of small country churches, important nature reserves and noteworthy prehistoric sites, as well as descriptions of castles, stately homes, museums and steam railways.

Whilst it is anticipated that most visitors will be travelling by motorcar to the places mentioned in the guide, there are several sites where walkers can gain ready access from the major walking routes outlined in the section on long-distance paths.

The countryside of East Sussex, with its downland hills, coastal cliffs and wealden woods, is one of the most beautiful areas of the south of England. Its proximity to London, however, makes it vulnerable to the development of commuter towns and villages that can be at odds with a predominantly rural area.

Visitors and locals can play a part in protecting this country environment against excessive development by joining an appropriate conservation or heritage body, such as those mentioned in this guide. Membership of such organisations gives free entry to their sites, and usually represents very good value. It also enables members to make their voice heard in local and central government circles when conservation issues are debated.

Visitors can also help preserve the Sussex downland by respecting the Country Code, contributing an offering to the small country churches they visit, and making use of local services, such as the village pub.

We hope you will enjoy visiting many of the places mentioned in this guide, and will find our information helpful. To help make your reading more enjoyable, we have included a selection of line drawings of some of the most prominent sights in each section.

East Sussex has much to offer in its history, culture and landscape. Enjoy it!

Firefly Publications
www.fireflypublications.co.uk

Note:
For the companion guide to this edition, please ask your bookshop for our West Sussex Guide (ISBN 0-9515691-1-2).

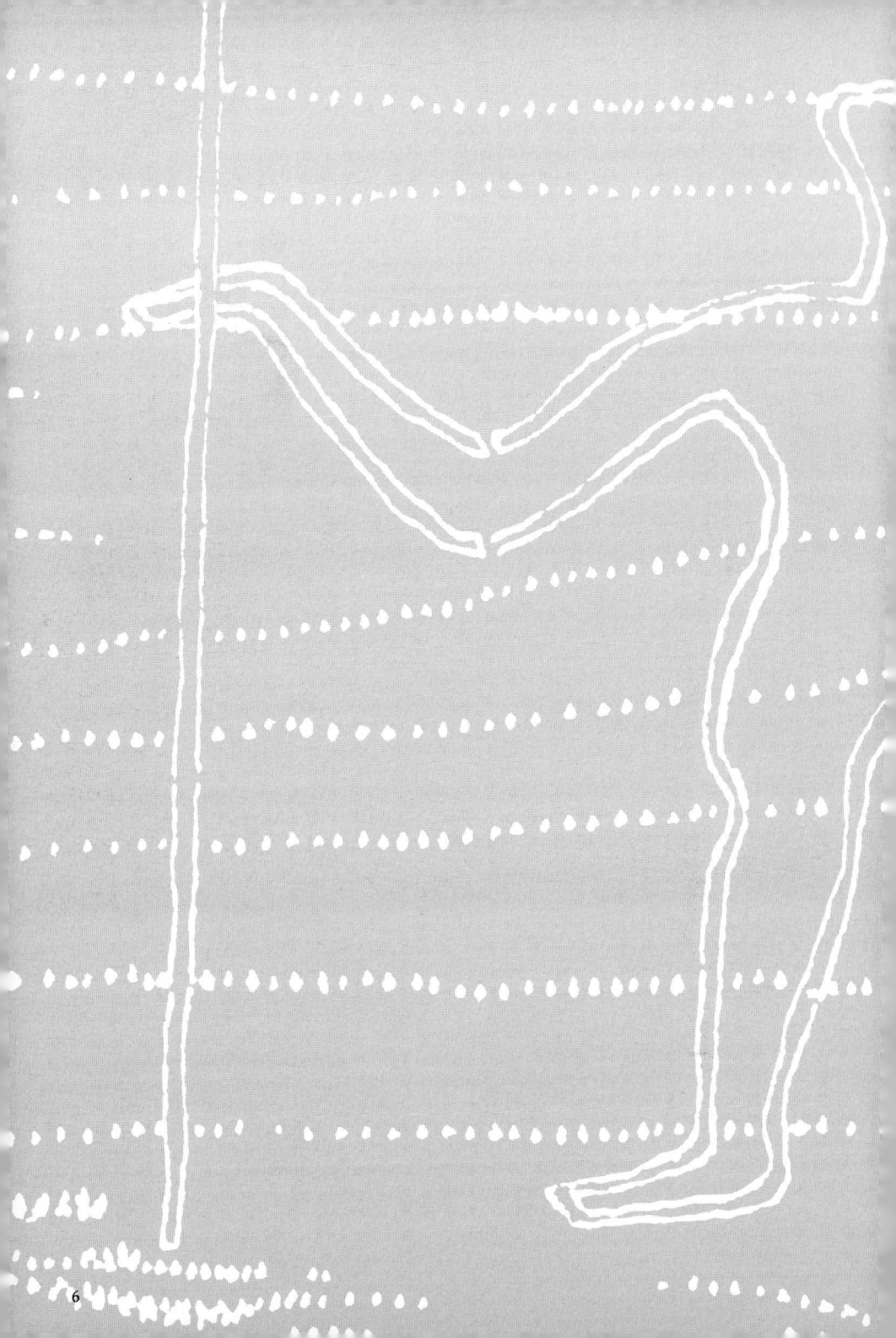

Prehistoric sites

Castle Hill, Seaford

Devil's Dyke

Ditchling Beacon

High Rocks

Wilmington - the Long Man

The Sussex Downs provide vivid evidence of human occupation going back some six thousand years when Neolithic farmers began clearing the hilltops for farming. Such was the mark made by these ancient predecessors that even today the visitor can see the outlines of burial mounds, ditches, early field systems and the hill-forts that defended them in the centuries leading to the Roman occupation in 43AD. More intriguing still are monuments such as the Long Man at Wilmington, one of the few hill-carvings to be found in the South of England. Its date, however, is a source of heated debate. It could be prehistoric, but the earliest record of it is only about 1710. The most reliable evidence of prehistory is that obtained by archaeologists, whose finds of flints, pottery, metal implements, animal bones and, very occasionally, human remains can now be very accurately dated. The Downs in East Sussex have yielded a considerable number of such artefacts.

Castle Hill, Seaford

Excavations show that there was a downland settlement here around 1500BC made up of enclosures, trackways and boundaries. The inhabitants grew crops, farmed various animals and practised a range of rural crafts. Their dead were buried in Round Barrows, many of which can still be seen as grassy rounded humps on grassland or in the middle of ploughed fields. There was possibly an Iron Age hillfort here (c.400BC).

Access via seafront footpath signposted to Seaford Head.

Devil's Dyke

This portion of the Downs to the north of Hove contains one of the later Iron Age hill-forts (c.100BC-43AD). The origins of man-made activity in this area go back much earlier to at least the Bronze Age (c.1000BC) when the Downs were divided into localities by means of cross-ridge dykes, often incorporating natural features. The height of the hill is over 700 feet (217m) and gives magnificent views northwards across the Weald. The Dyke itself is a natural ravine. It achieved its name from an early legend that tells the story that the Devil wished to cut off the area from the advance of Christianity from the east and built the dyke as an obstacle.

Refreshments may be obtained from the restaurant and bar situated at the top of the unclassified road leading to the dyke viewing points.

Access via the A27 at Blatchington or from A23 at Pyecombe.

Ditchling Beacon

This site with its spectacular views north and east is a favourite spot for locals as well as for visitors. It is the highest spot on the eastern section of the Downs at over 800 feet (248m). It is known to have been a hill-fort in the early Iron Age (c.1000-400BC). At the time of the Spanish Armada in 1588, the crest was topped by a large beacon to give warning of the invaders. There are wonderful views northwards.

The area is now owned by the National Trust, who were given the land by Sir Stephen Demitriadi in memory of his son, F.O. Richard Demitriadi, who was shot down in his Hurricane during the Battle of Britain in August 1940.

The site contains a nature reserve managed by the Sussex Wildlife Trust. Items of interest include rare chalkland plants, such as the Fragrant Orchid, and birds such as the Skylark and Kestrel.

The Beacon can be reached via the A27 at Hollingbury or from the direction of Ditchling village. Car park but no facilities.

High Rocks

On the western outskirts of Tunbridge Wells lies this collection of huge rock shelters dating back to the Mesolithic Age (c.4000BC). The site has yielded evidence of Iron Age pottery (c.400BC) and a possible hill-fort. These are spectacular rock formations for this part of southern England.

Access via A26 about one kilometre west of Tunbridge Wells.

Wilmington - the Long Man

As noted above, the date of this huge figure-in-outline is unknown. It could be prehistoric or much later (e.g. medieval). At more than 230 feet high (70m), it is the largest such figure in Europe, even larger than the Cerne Giant in Dorset. The earliest references to the Long Man suggest that the figure was originally outlined by depressions or shallow excavations in the chalk soil. In 1874 the outline was marked in yellow bricks, but these were replaced in the 1960's by concrete blocks. The figure is unusually elongated, which gives it a perspective that enables the viewer on the ground to see it as a stocky figure, whereas from the air it is much slimmer. The abundance of early sites, such as Neolithic flint mines and long barrows, Bronze Age round barrows and Iron Age coins in the immediate vicinity do not, as yet, show any reliable links between the figure and its setting. The mystery remains!

The figure is probably best viewed from the village of Wilmington in the vicinity of the church.

Access via the A27 at Wilmington west of Polegate.

The Long Man of Wilmington

Castles

Bodiam (NT)	
Camber (EH)	
Hastings	
Herstmonceux	
Lewes	
Newhaven Fort	
Pevensey (EH)	
Rye, Ypres Tower	
Winchelsea, Town Walls	

East Sussex is well endowed with castles, mostly built to protect the Channel ports, important to the economic life of the south since Roman times. Most of these castles are now in ruins. Only one, Pevensey, predates the Norman Conquest by any significant margin. Most were strong, defensive fortresses rather than fortified manor houses. The most elegant example, Herstmonceux, is the only one now occupied, while Newhaven fort serves as a military museum. The sturdy remains of Lewes Castle tower splendidly over the town, whilst Bodiam, perhaps the most romantic, with its perfect exterior and placid moat is an ideal location for any film director wishing to recreate a medieval atmosphere. Other fortifications include the remains of the castle at Hastings, and the town walls at Rye and Winchelsea. There is also the fortress built by Henry VIII at Camber near Rye. All these sites provide vivid evidence of Sussex life at different periods in its long history, spanning the Roman, Saxon, Norman, and early and late medieval periods, as well as later periods such as the time of Napoleon Bonaparte and World War II. Martello towers built during the Napoleonic Wars have not been included here, but appear under Museums.

Bodiam (NT)

This impressive building epitomises the romantic view of a medieval castle with its rounded turrets, sturdy walls and crenellated battlements surrounded by a neatly constructed moat. Seen from the outside it is everyone's idea of a picture postcard castle. It is thus somewhat disappointing to discover that there is very little left of the interior.

Completed in 1385 as a fortification against the marauding French by the local magnate, Sir Edward Dallyngrigge, it saw little military action. It was attacked in 1483 during the Wars of the Roses, but only fell into disrepair during the English Civil War, when it was partially dismantled by order of Oliver Cromwell. It was rescued by local MP, 'Mad Jack' Fuller at the beginning of the 19th century, and finally restored by Lord Curzon, who left it to the National Trust in 1926.

The Trust have provided a small museum to give an idea of what the castle may have looked like in its heyday.

Parking, WC and tea-room. Open daily mid Feb-Oct, 1000-1800, weekends Nov-mid Feb. Entrance: adult £3.70, child £1.85, family £9.25, free to NT members.

Access east of A21 between Robertsbridge and Hurst Green on minor road (2-3 miles), or via A229 about 2 miles south of Hawkhurst on the Hastings road.

Camber (EH)

This castle is a rare example of a Henrician fort, built overlooking the river Rother during the 16th century to protect the harbour at Rye. The substantial remains of the castle date from the 1540's, when Henry VIII spent considerable sums of money on strengthening the defences

Bodiam Castle

against possible attack by the Spanish.

By the early part of the 17th century the river had moved out of range of the castle's guns, and in 1642 the guns were taken to Rye and the castle was dismantled.

The main external structures remain, showing a massive central keep surrounded by an octagonal curtain wall with five huge D-shaped bastions on the outside.

Now in an isolated position it is only open 1 July-30 September. The site is managed on behalf of English Heritage by Rye Harbour Nature Reserve.

Entry: adult £2, child £1. Approach off A259 just east of Rye, signposted to Rye Harbour, then walk across open fields.

Hastings

The castle at Hastings dates from the time of the Norman Conquest in 1066.

So important a role did this site play in the heroic folklore of the Normans, that this was the first pre-Conquest castle to appear on the famous Bayeux tapestry.

The ruined church in the castle grounds was founded several years before the Conquest by Edward the Confessor as a collegiate community. At one time Thomas Becket was dean of the college in the 12th century.

In the latter part of the 13th century much of the bailey fell into the sea, and the castle ceased to function as a defensive position, becoming a centre for the clergy until the college was suppressed in the 1540's.

An informative audio-visual programme (English/French) covering the history of the castle is available throughout the day in a purpose-built theatre modelled on a medieval siege tent.

Open all year 1000-1700 (earlier in winter). Admission: adult £3.20, child £2.10, concessions £2.60, family £9.50. Vouchers available offering discount for visits to Smugglers Adventure.

The castle is sited on high ground overlooking the centre of the town.

Herstmonceux

This elegant building is a magnificent example of a late medieval fortified manor house, dating from 1441. Built for Sir Roger Fiennes, it was the first great building since Roman times to be constructed in brick. Partly dismantled in 1777, it was extensively restored in 1933, and in 1949 became the home of the Greenwich Observatory. The castle is not open to the public, as it is occupied as a Study Centre, but guided tours are available most days.

Set in 300 acres of woodland and gardens, and surrounded by a moat, Herstmonceux is a beautiful sight. The gardens and nature trail are open to the public daily between April and October from 1000-1800 (1700 October). Visitor centre, shop and tearoom available. Nature trail.

Admission (grounds): adult £3.50, child £2.70, concessions £2.70, family ticket £10.50. Guided tours extra. Joint tickets available for the Herstmonceux Science Centre (see Museums) close by.

Lewes

The origins of this impressive fortification date from the Norman Conquest when William de Warenne, one of William the Conqueror's key supporters, was granted the lands around Lewes. He established a motte and bailey castle on the present site in about 1077. Lewes castle formed part of a line of Norman forts stretching across Sussex, aimed at ensuring a clear route to London for the king, and adequate protection of his key Channel ports.

The original wooden stockade was replaced by massive stone walls and a shell keep later in the Norman period (early 12th century) by de Warenne's son. Towers were added to the keep later in the 13th century by the seventh earl. Then early in the 14th century the barbican entrance was built - its curved Gothic arch contrasting with the earlier rounded arches of the Norman builders.

Much of the keep remains today and there are wonderful views to the south across the town and the flood-plain of the river Ouse. The castle remains are in the care of the Sussex Archaeological Society, who also manage the adjacent Barbican museum (see Museums).

Open daily 1000-1730 (or dusk). Admission (Castle and museum): adult £4, child £2, concessions £3.50. Combined tickets also available, giving admission to Anne of Cleves House (see Stately Homes).

Newhaven Fort

This harbour fortress was built by the Victorians in the 1860's to protect the harbour of Newhaven.

During World War II it was used as the headquarters of the Canadian forces before the ill-fated Dieppe Raid in August 1942. In a quiet corner of the complex is a simple memorial to the many Canadians who died during that fearsome landing more than 50 years ago.

The fort is now a major military museum covering some 10 acres with exhibits ranging from Napoleonic times to the Second World War. Of particular interest are the displays dealing with the Dieppe Raid, D-Day, and life on the Home Front during World War II.

Open daily from 1 April to end of October, 1030-1800. Admission: adult £3.95, child £2.50, concessions £3.50, family ticket £12.50.

Pevensey

These extensive ruins date back to Roman times when the fort of Anderida was built (c.290AD) to protect the Bay of Pevensey. The flint rubble walls of the Roman fort still provide the external boundaries of the castle. The Normans took over the old fort in 1066 after the Battle of Hastings and began to transform it into a major stronghold using the eastern end of the site.

Today we can still see substantial remains of the 12th century gatehouse, keep and postern linked by the massive

Pevensey Castle

13th century walls and towers, which enclose the inner bailey or courtyard. The remains of the keep are insufficient to show what the finished building may have looked like, but its unusual shape is quite unique. During World War II it was fitted with a machine-gun post, which can still be seen from the ground. The towers are quite well preserved, and the North tower has some vaulting in its basement. The 360° views from the top of the curtain walls give an idea of the military importance of the site, which dominates the local area. In the inner bailey is a sixteenth century Tudor cannon dating from the time of Queen Elizabeth I.

The site is well-maintained by English Heritage. There is a warden on site, and tape-recorded guides and booklets are available. Tea rooms. Entrance: adult £2.50, child £1.30, concessions £1.90. Open all year 1000-1800 (1600 in winter).

Approach via A259 at Pevensey and follow signs.

Rye

The Ypres Tower at Rye is not so much a castle as a fortified part of the town walls. The tower dates from about 1249 and the walls from 1329. In its heyday in the 15th century, Rye was a prosperous port, one of the Cinque Ports, and a market town exporting wool and iron abroad. The Ypres tower gets its name not from the famous World War I battlefield in Flanders, but from the person who purchased it in 1430, one John de Ypres.

As the coastline changed and Rye found itself some distance from the sea, its prosperity declined. Today, with its half-timbered buildings and many cobbled streets, it is still reckoned to be one of the finest examples of a medieval port in Britain.

The town is located on the A259 between Hastings and Ashford. The Ypres Tower is open daily from April - October 1030-1730. Admission: adult £1.50, child £0.50p.

Winchelsea (Town Walls)

Winchelsea was given royal authority to build its walls in 1283, when the king (Edward I) intended to found a new town to replace an earlier one to the east, which had been swept away by the sea. Like its neighbour, Rye, Winchelsea was one of the original Cinque Ports. It, too, became similarly isolated from the sea and thus redundant. The various medieval towers are still impressive, especially the Strand Gate, the Pipewell Gate and the New Gate. These are all early 15th century in style.

Other sites of interest include the Court Hall and St. Thomas' Church (see Churches).

Winchelsea lies on the A259 between Hastings and Rye.

Churches, Abbeys and Priories

Alfriston - St Andrew's

Battle Abbey (EH)

Battle - St Mary's

Bayham Abbey (EH)

Berwick - St Michael & All Angels

Bexhill - St Peter

Bishopstone - St Andrew

Brede - St George's

Brighton, Preston Park - St Peter

Ditchling - St Margaret

Etchingham - The Assumption & St Nicholas

Fletching - St Andrew & St Mary the Virgin

Heron's Ghyll - St John the Evangelist

Herstmonceux - All Saints

Horsted Keynes - St Giles

Jevington - St Andrew

Lewes - St Anne

Lewes - St Pancras

Lewes Priory

Lindfield - All Saints

Lullington - The Good Shepherd

Mayfield - St Dunstan

Mayfield - Old Palace Chapel

Michelham Priory

Mountfield - All Saints

Piddinghoe Church

Plumpton - St Michael & All Angels

Rotherfield - St Denys

Rye - St Anthony of Padua

Rye - St Mary

Southease Church

Wadhurst - St Peter & St Paul

West Firle - St Peter

Wilmington - St Mary & St Peter

Winchelsea - St Thomas

East Sussex abounds with interesting churches. We have selected mostly village churches, although there are a few town churches where these are of special note. The county contains the ruins of several outstanding examples of the religious houses that dominated much of ordinary life in medieval England. These are notably at Lewes, Michelham, Battle and Bayham. There is also the Great Hall at the Old Palace at Mayfield, once the residence of the medieval archbishops of Canterbury. The hall is now the stunning chapel of a convent school. Apart from the redundant church at Preston Park, Brighton, all the parish churches we have described still have active congregations, whose presence ensures that many precious sites of English history and culture are cared for, and remain open to visitors. Most of these churches are more than 700 years old. They are still primarily places of prayer and reflection, and only secondly repositories of English history. It is always helpful to leave a donation, however modest, to enable a small country parish to continue to keep its church open for worshipper and visitor alike. The fabric of these ancient churches is part of our national heritage, and we ought to contribute something towards the upkeep of the places we visit, as we do when we visit a stately home or local museum.

Alfriston - St. Andrews

Sometimes referred to as 'the cathedral of the Downs', this imposing flintwork church dates from about 1360, although there was certainly an earlier church on the site. Its cruciform shape is fairly uncommon. The central tower has a single broached spire. In medieval times the transepts were chapels in their own right, the south chapel being the Lady chapel.

On the south wall of the chancel are particularly richly-decorated examples of a sedilia and piscina, dating from the 15th century. On the opposite side is an unusual Easter Sepulchre with carvings above. A most uncommon sight here also is the presence on the chancel's easternmost beam of the hooks that in pre-Reformation times were used to hold the Lenten veil over the altar and tabernacle during Lent. There is some medieval glass in the church, notably in the windows of the north transept. The remaining glass is Victorian, some of it by C.E.Kempe. The plain square font mounted on a pedestal with octagonal shafts pre-dates the church.

The church overlooks a beautiful stretch of the Cuckmere river at the rear, whilst close by is the Clergy House (see Stately Homes and Gardens).

Alfriston lies midway between the A27 Lewes to Polegate road and the A259 Seaford to Eastbourne road. The church stands in a prominent position at the southern end of the village to the east of the road.

Battle Abbey

The substantial remains of this famous Benedictine abbey established by William the Conqueror after the battle of Hastings in 1066 are divided between a school and an English Heritage site. The school is housed in the main house of the former abbey, whilst English Heritage care for the imposing gatehouse and the substantial remains of the former monks' dormitory. The abbey church itself was razed to the ground in 1538 following the suppression of the monastery by Henry VIII. Only a few crypt chapels remain. Tradition has it that the original High Altar was sited at the spot where the Saxon King Harold fell during the battle. All that is left today is a plaque to mark the place. Several of the abbey's remains, such as the dormitory and novices' library, however, provide a glimpse of what they may have looked like in their heyday.

The museum display in the gatehouse gives a very informative account of life in the medieval abbey, and is well worth a visit, so long as you can manage the steep, narrow stairs.

Admission: adult £4.30, child £2.20, concessions £3.20. Family ticket £10.80.

The abbey entrance lies at the eastern end of Battle high street. Access from the A21 onto the A2100 north of Hastings.

Battle Abbey

Battle - St. Mary's

This fascinating church was founded in the early 12th century by the serving abbot to cater for the needs of the growing local community. There are some excellent early 14th century wall-paintings, a Norman font with a 15th century painted cover, and a fine example of a 16th century alabaster tomb, dedicated to Sir Anthony Browne and his wife. Browne, who was Henry VIII's Master of the Horse, was the beneficiary of the abbey upon the Dissolution. The church also contains an unusual Breeches Bible. The building lies just round the corner from the present abbey gatehouse.

Bayham Abbey

The ruins of this early 13th century abbey founded in 1208 on the Kent border by the Premonstratensian (White) canons are among the most evocative in Sussex. This site, like Battle, was also once in the possession of Sir Anthony Browne following the Dissolution of the monasteries, and is now in the care of English Heritage.

The gardens were developed in the 19th century under the supervision of the famous landscape architect, Humphry Repton. Part of the Georgian Dower House is also open to the public.

Open daily from 1000-1800 (1600 in winter). Admission: adult £2.20, child £1.10, concessions £1.70.

Bayham is situated to the south-east of Tunbridge Wells, turning south off the A21.

Berwick - St Michael & All Angels

This much-altered medieval church is best known for its striking wall-paintings, undertaken during World War II by members of the Bloomsbury group, notably Duncan Grant and Vanessa and Quentin Bell, who lived at the nearby Charleston Farmhouse (see Stately Homes). The paintings were done on plaster board, pre-cut to fit the nave arches and other locations in the church. Subjects depicted include Christ in Glory, the Annunciation, and the Supper at Emmaus, where the models for the two disciples were Australian Air Force men serving in Sussex during the war.

There is a most unusual stone font, probably Saxon, built into the 12th century pillar on the south west corner of the nave.

Berwick lies to the south of the A27 between Selmeston and Polegate. The church is reached about 400 metres past the Cricketers' Inn.

Bexhill - St Peter

Although much of this church was massively restored during the Victorian age, it still shows evidence of its ancient past, mainly in its Norman tower and part of the nave. The north chapel is a chantry chapel dating from the 15th century. One of the most interesting features is the Saxon coffin lid discovered during the restoration work and now located on the tower wall together with a large 13th century carved grave-slab.

The church is situated in the Old Town area of modern Bexhill. Access via A259.

Bishopstone - St Andrew

This little church of Saxon origins is one of the oldest in the county. The nave and porch are Saxon, while the distinctive tower is Norman (early 12th century). The south wall has an unusual Mass-dial with the name EADRIC on it.

Bishopstone Church

Inside the north aisle and south arch show typical Norman chevron and dog-toothing work. There is an early English arch between nave and chancel. The square font is Norman.

Access via A259 on the outskirts of Seaford between Seaford and Newhaven.

If locked, details of where key may be obtained are posted on door.

Brede - St George's

The present building dates from the late 12th century, including the nave, but is mostly 15th century. The chancel is Perpendicular in style, and would have included a rood loft and screen in those times. The remains of the loft can be seen above the present pulpit.

The Lady Chapel contains a 15th century tomb to Robert Oxenbridge (d.1487), and a later, and much grander tomb, to his son, Sir Goddard Oxenbridge (d.1531). Goddard was apparently a very tall man, known as 'the Brede Giant'. Another interesting feature in this chapel is the statue of the Madonna, carved out of a solid piece of oak by Clare Sheridan, a first cousin of Sir Winston Churchill, in 1941.

The 14th century octagonal font is interesting, being decorated with four heraldic shields depicting the Holy Spirit, and the Latin blessing *'In nomine Patris'* used at baptism.

There is also a display case which includes an early copy (1705) of 'The Imitation of Christ' by Thomas a Kempis, and a so-called 'Vinegar Bible' (1717), because the word 'vineyard' at the head of the page was misspelt.

Brede church lies on the south side of the village along the A28 between Hastings and Broad Oak.

Brighton - St Peter, Preston Park

This little gem of a church on the outskirts of Brighton is now in the care of the Redundant Churches Fund, having no parish community.

The flint building is mostly 13th century. It once had extensive medieval wall-paintings, of which some still survive and are well worth seeing. There is an unusual altar based on the tomb chest of Edward Eldrington, who was lord of the manor in the early 16th century. If the church is locked, information about keyholders is posted in the porch.

The church lies just east of the main A23 London road at Preston Park north of the town centre.

Ditchling - St Margaret

The nave is the earliest part of this handsome church, dating from the late 11th century. The chancel and south transept are late 13th century, and the former has some fine stonework. The east window is an excellent example of intricate Geometrical style (14C). The south chapel is early 14th century and contains a fine Decorated window with tracery. There is also a good example of an Elizabethan memorial dedicated to one Henry Poole (1580).

The church is situated on the Keymer road near the busy village crossroads.

Etchingham - The Assumption & St Nicholas

The present church dates from the 14th century. Despite its rather plain exterior, evidence of its Cistercian foundation, there is plenty of interest within, notably the flowing window tracery reckoned to be the best in Sussex, the late 14th century/early 15th century brasses, and the misericords in the chancel seats. The chancel is longer than the nave, typical of a church where a religious order was once present.

There are still remnants of medieval glass in the windows, and the weathervane is the oldest in Sussex. The village is situated on the A265 between Burwash and Hurst Green, and the church lies just to the north of the road near the railway station.

Fletching - St Andrew & St Mary the Virgin

This spacious cruciform church has a wealth of interesting features. Apart from the tower which is early Norman, the building dates mainly from the 13th century. The graceful octagonal spire, one of the

highest in the county, dates from the 14th century. The nave is mainly Early English, but the doorway from the tower into the nave indicates an earlier Norman arch with chevron carving.

The chancel is surprisingly long and wide compared with the nave, suggesting the presence of a religious order, but this did not happen before 1398, when Fletching was made over to the prior of Michelham. The lancet windows and east window are late 13th century. The stained glass is Victorian, mostly by John Kemp. The rood screen is in the Perpendicular style, early 14th century.

There is a very fine 14th century brass of Sir Walter Dalyngrygge and his wife in the south transept, together with an excellent example of an Elizabethan alabaster tomb chest of a former High Sheriff, Richard Leche and his wife. Another interesting feature here is the brass to one Peter Denot, a glover, who took part in the Cade rebellion against Henry VI in 1450.

Fletching Church

Chroniclers say that Simon de Montfort and his men prayed here *en route* to the battle of Lewes in 1264.

The famous eighteenth century historian, Gibbon, who wrote the *Decline and Fall of the Roman Empire*, is buried in the Sheffield family mausoleum located in the north transept.

Fletching lies north-west of the A272 between Newick and Maresfield.

Heron's Ghyll - St John the Evangelist

The origins of this isolated little Roman Catholic church are unusual. The house (Heron's Ghyll) was bought in 1879 by the then Duke of Norfolk from the pre-Raphaelite poet, Coventry Patmore, who had become a Catholic later in life. In 1891 the property came into the hands of the Duke's nephew, James Hope, Deputy Speaker in the House of Commons, and later Lord Rankeillour of Buxted. He decided to build a church here in place of an earlier iron chapel.

The new church was formally opened in September 1897, when the preacher was Cardinal Vaughan. The windows and font were given by members of the Norfolk and Hope families. A thriving parish community is present today.

The church lies to the east of the main A26 road between Uckfield and Tunbridge Wells.

Herstmonceux - All Saints

This earliest part of this ancient church is the late 12th century tower, which unusually spans the western end of the nave and its north aisle. The nave, chancel and aisles are 13th and 14th century. Later changes came in the 15th century when the north chapel and the east wall of the sanctuary were built in the same brick used for the construction of the nearby castle. There is an excellent example of medieval art in the early 16th century Dacre tomb with its

Decorated Gothic canopy and beautifully carved figures of Lord Dacre (d.1533) and his son in Caen stone.

There is a plain 14th century stone font, and, set in the floor of the chancel aisle, covered by a mat, a large brass of Sir Wm. Fiennes (d.1402).

The church is located some two miles to the south of the A271 on the eastern side of the village between Herstmonceux and Windmill Hill.

Horsted Keynes - St Giles

This fascinating church lies just across the border in West Sussex. Little remains of the original Norman church, which was mostly rebuilt in the 13th century. The nave, chancel and south transept are all of this period. The tower crossing provides the main evidence of the Norman building, where three of the four arches are of 12th century origin.

One of the most unusual sights in the church is to be found in the north wall of the chancel, where there is a small recess with an effigy of a tiny Crusader knight. It is likely that the little shrine contains the heart of the unknown Crusader who died sometime in the mid-13th century. The north wall also contains a marble coffin lid with a clearly-defined cross along its length. It is early 14th century and may have been part of the tomb of the Prior of Lewes. The plain octagonal font is 15th century, and the north door adjacent to it is late Saxon/ early Norman. It was moved stone by stone to its present position when the church was enlarged in Victorian times.

The church was used regularly for worship by Harold Macmillan, Earl of Stockton, and former Prime Minister, who died in 1986. A plaque in memory of him and his wife, Dorothy, is located on the north aisle wall.

Situated to the north of the village along

Church Lane, the church is not easily visible from the main road. The village can be accessed via the A275 at Danehill or via the B2028 just south of Ardingly. The Bluebell Railway runs close by.

Jevington - St Andrew

This ancient church has Saxon origins, which are evident in the construction of the tower (c.900-950), including the use of Roman bricks set herring-bone style in the massive walls. There is a very rare Saxon relief of the Risen Christ set into the north wall of the nave, possibly part of an ancient mural or a rood-screen.

The nave is mostly late 15th century with Perpendicular style windows and an excellent example of a Tudor wagon roof. The chancel arch is 13th century, and is pierced on either side by squints, enabling people seated on the outer pews in the nave to see the elevation of the Host at Mass. The original squints would have been more angled than the restored versions completed in the 1870's. The east window is 13th century and has noticeable splaying, giving the effect of a much larger window. The font dates from about 1400.

Jevington may be reached off the A27 at Polegate near Eastbourne.

Lewes - St Anne

Situated well outside the original town walls, this 12th century church stands in a dominant position on the western approach to Lewes. The tower, nave and south chapel are Norman. There is a notable four-bay arcade dating from the end of the 12th century, and a fine Norman font, almost barrel-shaped and with basketweave decoration. The chancel south wall has the remains of a medieval squint, enabling a priest at a side chapel to synchronise his celebration of Mass with the principal celebrant at the High Altar. A gallery was built in the 18th century at the west end of the nave, and this has the coat of arms of George IV displayed on it.

On the opposite side of the road to St Anne's is the Victorian church of **St Pancras**, built for the worship of Lewes's growing number of Roman Catholics in 1870. The strong allegiance of Lewes to the Protestant cause severely restricted the practising of Catholicism in the town, and there were riots at the opening of the church. The wounds to the community from Tudor times, when eleven Protestants were burned at the stake in 1557, have taken centuries to heal. Even today the Bonfire night (November 5) celebrations in the town still include 'No Popery' banners, to the embarrassment of most fellow Christians.

Lewes Priory

At the height of its powers this Cluniac foundation exerted a huge influence on the surrounding area. Founded in 1077 by William de Warenne, one of William the Conqueror's senior lieutenants, the priory church of St.Pancras was once larger than Chichester cathedral. The church and its monastic buildings are now but pathetic remnants of their past glory. The ugly wire fence surrounding the main site only serves to emphasise the sense of doom that pervades these ruins.

Just alongside the public footpath is a fine modern sculpture some six feet high in the form of a knight's helmet. This is a memorial of the 700th anniversary of the Battle of Lewes, 1264, fought between Simon de Montfort and King Henry III. The king lost the battle and was obliged to sign a treaty known as the *Mise of Lewes*, in which he conceded that his taxation demands should be subject to the consent of a form of Parliament. Thereafter, towns such as Lewes were entitled to send two representatives to Parliament until the reforms of 1867. The sculpture was designed by

Enzo Plazzotta and presented by Sir Tufton Beamish, M.P. in 1964.

Access free at any time from Southover High Street.

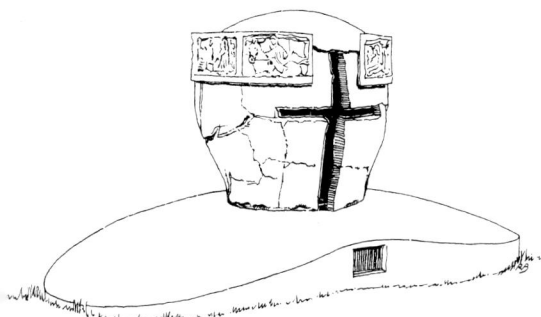

Battle of Lewes Monument

Lindfield - All Saints

The village of Lindfield was once a great centre of ironworking in the mid-Sussex area, and its church reflects the prosperity of that trade in medieval times. Although in West Sussex, Lindfield is on a popular visitor route out of the commuter town of Haywards Heath, and is included here. All Saints was built mostly in the 13th and 14th centuries. The impressive nave has arcaded aisles built in the Decorated style - one of the later forms of Gothic. The chancel also has arcades, this time in the Perpendicular style - the most refined period of Gothic architecture. The east window with its flowing tracery is Decorated, and is comparable to that at Etchingham (see above).

The church has two transepts. The font is Tudor (c.1530). There are numerous brasses and other memorials, the oldest of which is the brass of one Richard Challoner (d.1501). The two-storey porch (14thC) is unusual. Note the Mass dials on either side.

The church lies at the north end of the village on the B2028 between Haywards Heath and Ardingly.

Lullington - The Good Shepherd

This truly is a little church, measuring only some sixteen feet square! It nevertheless can hold some twenty worshippers. What remains is basically part of the chancel of a 13th century church, which once belonged to Battle Abbey.

There are five lancet windows, one on the north side dating from the 13th century, and the other four from the 14th century. The church was restored in 1894, and is now dedicated to the Good Shepherd. Its original dedication is unknown.

The church is sited on high ground overlooking the Cuckmere river and the neighbouring church of St Andrew at Alfriston. It can be reached on foot from Alfriston, or by car from the unclassified Wilmington to Litlington road.

Mayfield - St Dunstan

St Dunstan, the 10th century archbishop of Canterbury, was born in this attractive wealden village. The tower of the present building dates from the 13th century, but after a major fire most of the church was rebuilt in the 15th and 16th centuries in the Perpendicular style. The nave has arcades typical of this style, making for loftiness and light. The wooden arch between the nave and the chancel is 16th century and is a rare example of linenfold carving.

As at Lindfield there is a two-storey porch, the top part forming a private oratory. The octagonal font is 17th century and the carved wooden pulpit is Jacobean. The wall monument near the entrance is Elizabethan, and there are two fine 18th century chandeliers in the nave. Also in the nave are two interesting iron grave slabs, dated 1668 and 1708, relating to the Sands family.

Mayfield, like Lewes, saw its share of Catholic backlash under Queen Mary, when four Protestants were burned at the stake. The memories of those days are revisited by the bonfire society that still operates in the village.

The church is situated centrally behind the village post office.

Mayfield - Old Palace Chapel

Just along from the parish church is the former palace of the archbishops of Canterbury, restored in the 1860's with the help of the then Duchess of Leeds, an American. The magnificent medieval Great Hall of the former palace is now the chapel of the Convent of the Holy Child Jesus, endowed by the duchess in 1872. It is one of the finest examples of a medieval hall in the country. The wide span of the 14th century stone arches with their remarkably preserved carvings provides a stunning setting for the school chapel.

There are six huge windows each thirty feet high with intricate carving. One small section of the east wall behind the statue of the Madonna and Child displays the medieval diaper carving that would once have covered the entire wall.

The statue of the Madonna is 14th century, possibly English. The painted crucifix suspended over the present high altar is also 14th century but Italian.

The last Catholic archbishop to reside at Mayfield was William Warham, who died in 1532, about the time of Henry VIII's divorce proceedings. This left the way clear for Thomas Cranmer, who, appointed by the king not by the Pope, sanctioned the divorce that brought about the break with Rome that has lasted ever since.

Entry to the chapel is through the 16th century gatehouse off the village street.

Mayfield is on the A267 between Heathfield and Tunbridge Wells.

Michelham Priory

Founded by the Black (Augustinian) Canons in 1292, the priory church of Our Lady was razed to the ground in 1537 at the Dissolution of the monasteries under Henry VIII. Some of the original community buildings survive and are in the care of the Sussex Archaeological Society.

The visitor is met by a fortified gatehouse (late 14th century) and a bridge over the moat. The principal priory house is now a museum of medieval and Tudor life. There is a physic garden full of plants used for medicinal purposes, a fish pond, a huge 16th century barn and lovely gardens, all surrounded by the largest water-filled medieval moat in England.

Michelham Priory

There is a working watermill, which still grinds flour in the traditional manner. This is one of the most attractive sites in the county.

Open March to October, Wednesday-Sunday only (every day in August). Shop and tearoom. Admission: adult £4.70, child £2.30, concessions £4, family £11.50.

Access via the A22 north of Polegate, or via A27, turning north at Berwick roundabout.

Mountfield - All Saints

This sturdy little church is from the Norman period with later additions. The nave and chancel are early 12th century, and there are the faded remains of medieval wall-paintings on the chancel arch. The earliest date from the 12th century, while the masonry patterns are late 13th century, overlaid with 14th century IHC monograms. It is also possible to read the fragments of the text of the Ten Commandments painted after the Protestant Reformation (late 16th century).

Unusually there are two squints, one on either side of the chancel arch, enabling people in the nave to see the elevation of the Host during Mass in pre-Reformation times. The large, round font, carved out of a single stone, is Norman with later (15th century) decorations.

The church may be reached west from the A2100 about halfway between Battle and Robertsbridge.

Piddinghoe Church

This attractive flint church overlooking the Ouse water-meadows dates from the Norman period. The nave and distinctive round tower are early 12th century. There is an intriguing carved stone face - possibly of Christ - projecting from the north aisle wall. Its provenance is unknown. The north arcades are in typically rounded Norman style, while the south arcades are Gothic. The tower is unusual, one of only three round towers in Sussex. It is surmounted by a weathervane in the form of a gilded sea-trout.

The chancel is early 13th century and has a fine arch with triple shafts. The deeply-recessed lancet windows topped by a round window (oculus) behind the altar are unusual for an east window. The square font is late 13th century. An interesting modern addition to the church is the rather striking mosaic of St John the Evangelist executed for the parish by Ann Clark.

If locked, the key may be obtained from the owner of the house facing the church entrance.

The hamlet of Piddinghoe is just north of Newhaven on the unclassified road running between Lewes and Newhaven.

Plumpton - St Michael & All Angels

This church is one of four Sussex churches with visible remains of early medieval wall-painting (frescoes) discovered in 1955. Unfortunately, most of the subjects were destroyed during the Victorian restorations in the 1870's. However, a few motifs remain, including a picture of Christ in the New Jerusalem, together with some of the best examples of medieval scroll work in the south of England.

From the early 12th century up to the 16th English churches were usually plastered and painted. Bare stonework was regarded as crude in those days. After the Reformation, when interior decoration and statues had to be removed, the reformers insisted on the display (in English) of the 'Sentences', notably the Ten Commandments, the Creed and the Lord's Prayer. These appear on boards on the west wall of the Norman nave. The chancel and tower are 13th century.

Plumpton is situated on the B2116 about halfway between Ditchling and Lewes. The church is located alongside the Agricultural College.

Rotherfield - St Denys

There are numerous pre- and post-Reformation artefacts in this mainly 13th century sandstone church. There are some outstanding examples of medieval wall-painting, primarily on the chancel arch. The single iron graveslab inside the church is unusual in that it has no inscription. It is thought to be 14th or 15th century. The canopied pulpit is 17th century, and the box pews 19th century.

The east window in the chancel is in

the Perpendicular style, but the glass is 19th century by William Morris to a design by Burne-Jones. The 13th century sedilia and piscina on the south wall of the chancel are excellent examples of their type. There are fragments of medieval glass in the Nevill chapel windows.

The octagonal stone font is probably Norman and was recovered from a nearby field little more than a century ago. The unusually tall wooden font cover has the date 1533 carved in one of its panels.

The church is located in the centre of the village on the B2100 to the east of Crowborough.

Rye - St Anthony of Padua
This little church was formally opened on 30 June 1929, fulfilling a pledge by the parish priest, Fr. Bonaventure, that if he survived the First World War, where he served as a chaplain in the Black Watch, he would build a church in honour of St Anthony. The parish had been in the hands of the Franciscans (Greyfriars) since 1910, when Fr. Bonaventure took over the former church of St Walburga, which had proved too small for the growing Catholic population at that time.

The church is a miniature basilica built in a Spanish-Romanesque style. Of particular note are the marble altar and pulpit, the stained glass windows and the Stations of the Cross in oak.

The church is located in Watchbell Street.

Rye - St Mary
This is one of the largest churches in Sussex. The nave and chancel are spacious and light. The oldest features, dating from the early 12th century, are the walls of the transepts and the crossing, and there is a fine example of a narrow Norman arch to the right of the North Door as you enter.

The nave is late 12th century, the Clare chapel is mostly 13th century, and the chancel pillars are 15th century.

The many architectural changes are evidence of the building's suffering in time of war. The worst damage was caused at the hands of the French in 1377, when the church was set on fire.

The church clock is a feature in its own right. The clock face on the north side of the tower is 18th century, but the clock's mechanism is 16th century. The 18ft pendulum can be seen from the central crossing inside the church.

The church is located on high ground close to the town centre.

Southease Church
Like its neighbour at Piddinghoe, this ancient little church also has a round tower dating from the early 12th century. The present church is developed around the nave of the original building. The earlier chancel and its aisles disappeared sometime between the 13th and 14th centuries. There is evidence of a painted medieval rood-screen (15th century) behind the present chancel arch. There are some very faded medieval wall paintings on the north and west walls of the nave. The restored font is late 12th century. The two church bells are medieval, one dating from 1280 is among the oldest in Sussex.

Southease is located midway between Lewes and Newhaven on the unclassified road that links them.

Wadhurst - St Peter & St Paul
This large church was a product of the Wealden iron industry in medieval times. Its origins go back to the 8th century when a church was founded by Duke Bertoald in 792AD. The earliest feature of the present building is the Norman tower, but most of the church is 14th century. The circular font is earlier, from the 13th century. The huge oak beams of the nave roof are probably 15th century.

The unique feature of the church, however, is the number of iron graveslabs set in the floor - more than any other church in England. They are all 17th and 18th century, and are as much a comment on different ways of spelling the same word as they are of the artistry of the makers.

The triptych painting of the Risen Christ ('I am the Resurrection and the Life') commemorates the men of the village who died in the Second World War. It was inspired by an Italian Renaissance painter, Andrea del Castagno. The glass in the 15th century window above the painting depicts Christ in glory and commemorates those who fell in the First World War.

Wadhurst church lies towards the south-eastern end of the village just off the B2099 to Ticehurst. Bewl Water is close by.

West Firle - St Peter
This village church is a history lesson in its own right with architectural features and artefacts ranging from the 13th to the 20th centuries. The north doorway is Norman, the chancel is 13th century, the nave arcades (Decorated) are 14th century, and the aisles are 15th century. There are well-preserved memorial brasses now displayed on the east wall of the north aisle, including the Bolney brass (15thC), and several relating to the Gage family. There is a 16th century chapel containing the impressive alabaster tomb of Sir John Gage, and a John Piper window depicting the Tree of Life.

The church lies at the eastern end of the village, and is approached off the main A27 at Firle to the east of Lewes.

Wilmington - St Mary & St Peter
Built to serve the parish, as well as the Benedictine Priory whose remaining buildings are now in the care of the Landmark Trust, this ancient church dates from Norman times. The chancel used by the monks has unusually splayed walls and dates from the 12th century. The nave, which was for the people, is 14th century.

Items of interest include the small stone figure, possibly of the Virgin Mary, on the north wall of the chancel, and the original rood beam just to the east of the arch. The huge yew in the churchyard is probably a thousand years old.

The few remaining priory buildings are not open to the public, but one elegant and well-preserved section still stands out as a memorial to what was once a handsome monastery. There are good views of the Long Man (see above) from the car-park near the church.

Access south of the A27 at Wilmington just west of Polegate.

Winchelsea - St Thomas
This lovely church is considered to contain some of the the finest examples of the Decorated period in Sussex (c.1250-1350). Like its neighbour at Rye, the little town of Winchelsea, including its church, suffered terribly at the hands of the French in the 14th century. All that remains now are the chancel and side chapels, but these are huge and lofty.

Seal of Winchelsea

There are several magnificent medieval tombs and monuments with elaborate stonework. The earliest are those on the north wall, where there are three black marble figures that pre-date the church, and were probably rescued from the original church which was given over to the sea in the 12th century. The figures and canopies on the south wall form the Alard chantry, dating from the early 14th century. The carved heads on the canopies include those of King Edward I and his second wife, Margaret. The first tomb is believed to be that of Gervase Alard, who was Admiral of the Western Fleet under Edward.

There is a little medieval glass in the north window of the chancel, but the rest of the beautiful stained glass work is by Douglas Strachan (d.1950) the Scottish stained glass artist, whose work may be seen in the Hague (Palace of Peace), Edinburgh Castle (War Memorial), Glasgow Cathedral, St. Giles Cathedral, and St. Paul's in London.

At the Reformation the dedication of the church was changed from St Thomas of Canterbury to St Thomas the Apostle in conformity with the official demotion of Thomas Becket.

Winchelsea lies off the A259 between Hastings and Rye. The church is in a central position.

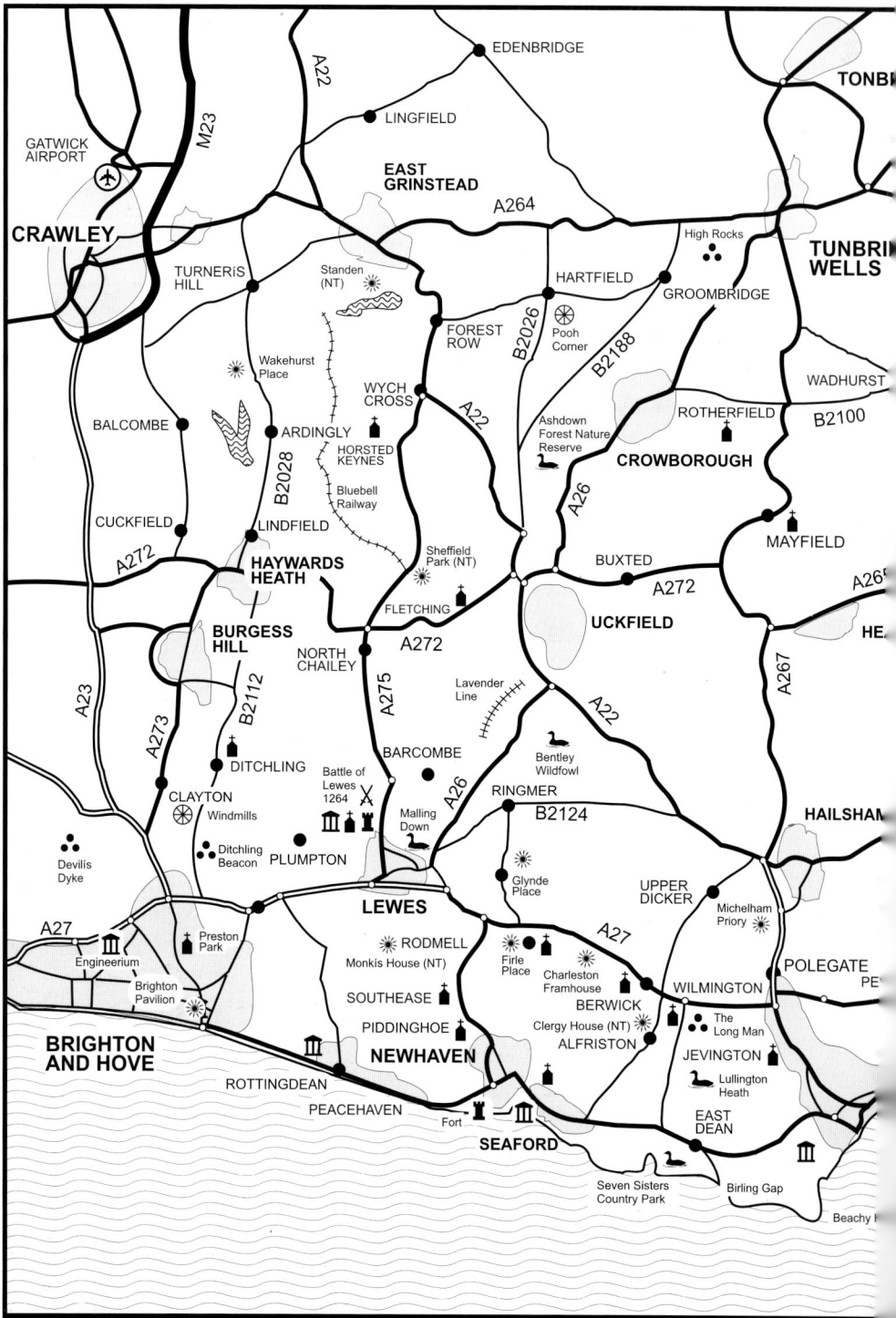

EDENBRIDGE

TONB[I]

A22

M23

LINGFIELD

GATWICK
AIRPORT

EAST
GRINSTEAD

A264

CRAWLEY

High Rocks

TUNBRI[
WELLS

TURNERiS
HILL

Standen
(NT)

HARTFIELD

GROOMBRIDGE

Wakehurst
Place

FOREST
ROW

B2026

Pooh
Corner

B2188

WADHURST

BALCOMBE

ARDINGLY

WYCH
CROSS

A22

Ashdown
Forest Nature
Reserve

ROTHERFIELD

B2100

HORSTED
KEYNES

CROWBOROUGH

CUCKFIELD

B2028

LINDFIELD

Bluebell
Railway

A26

MAYFIELD

A272

HAYWARDS
HEATH

Sheffield
Park (NT)

BUXTED

A272

UCKFIELD

A26[

BURGESS
HILL

FLETCHING

A272

HE[

A23

B2112

NORTH
CHAILEY

A275

Lavender
Line

A22

A267

A273

DITCHLING

BARCOMBE

Battle of
Lewes
1264

A26

Bentley
Wildfowl

RINGMER

HAILSHAM

CLAYTON

Windmills

Ditchling
Beacon

PLUMPTON

Malling
Down

B2124

Devilis
Dyke

Glynde
Place

UPPER
DICKER

Michelham
Priory

A27

LEWES

Engineerium

Preston
Park

RODMELL

Monkis House (NT)

Firle
Place

Charleston
Framhouse

A27

WILMINGTON

POLEGATE

PE[

Brighton
Pavilion

SOUTHEASE

BERWICK

The
Long Man

BRIGHTON
AND HOVE

PIDDINGHOE

NEWHAVEN

Clergy House (NT)

ALFRISTON

JEVINGTON

ROTTINGDEAN

PEACEHAVEN

Fort

Lullington
Heath

EAST
DEAN

SEAFORD

Seven Sisters
Country Park

Birling Gap

Beachy [

DGE

GE

GOUDHURST

LAMBERHURST

ham
ey

SISSINGHURST

CRANBROOK

A28

TENTERDEN

Bewl Water

A21

HAWKHURST

Kent & East
Sussex Railway

A259

TICEHURST

Pashley
House
Gardens

ETCHINGHAM

BODIAM
Castle (NT)

Great
Dixter

A268

Lamb
House

RYE

RWASH

NORTHIAM

Bateman's (NT)

CAMBER

FIELD

A21

SEDLESCOMBE

A28

Camber
Castle

A259

WINCHELSEA

Town Walls

BATTLE

Battle of
Hastings
1066

A259

FAIRLIGHT

A271

STMONCEUX

A259

HASTINGS

EY

BEXHILL

TBOURNE

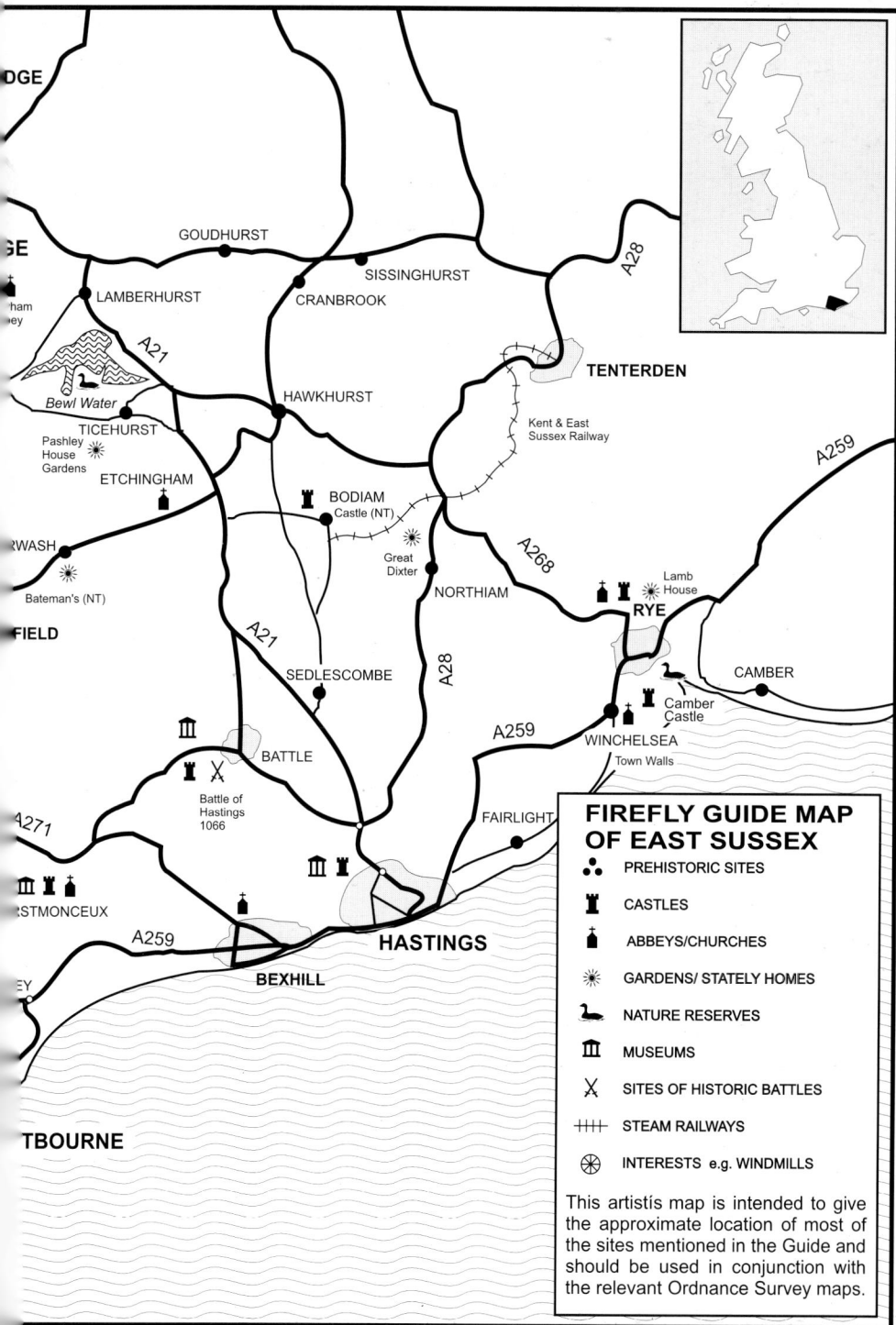

FIREFLY GUIDE MAP OF EAST SUSSEX

- PREHISTORIC SITES
- CASTLES
- ABBEYS/CHURCHES
- GARDENS/ STATELY HOMES
- NATURE RESERVES
- MUSEUMS
- X SITES OF HISTORIC BATTLES
- ┼┼┼┼ STEAM RAILWAYS
- INTERESTS e.g. WINDMILLS

This artistís map is intended to give the approximate location of most of the sites mentioned in the Guide and should be used in conjunction with the relevant Ordnance Survey maps.

Stately Homes and Gardens

Alfriston Clergy House (NT)

Batemans (NT)

Brighton Pavilion

Charleston Farmhouse

Firle Place

Glynde Place

Northiam, Great Dixter

Rodmell, Monk's House (NT)

Rye, Lamb House (NT)

Scotney Castle Garden (NT)

Sheffield Park (NT)

Standen (NT)

Ticehurst, Pashley Manor Gardens

Wakehurst Place (NT)

We have included a number of the most popular stately homes and other buildings of interest to visitors, as well as a small selection of public gardens, of which Wakehurst, Sheffield Park and Scotney Castle Garden are the outstanding examples. The National Trust bought its first property in East Sussex - the Clergy House at Alfriston. Its other properties in the county include Bateman's, where Rudyard Kipling lived for several years, and the Monk's House at Rodmell, where another writer, Virgina Woolf, lived until her death in 1941. There are no palaces in East Sussex, but several large manor houses, of which Firle, Glynde, Standen and Great Dixter are excellent examples. Most of the houses are closed during the winter months, but their gardens are often open all year round. Most provide ample car parking and refreshment facilities, as well as a shop.

Alfriston Clergy House (NT)

This thatched, timber-framed cottage was built in the 14th century as the priest's house for the parish church of St Andrew. It was the first building to be purchased for the National Trust in 1896, and is a fine example of a rare Wealden building.

Clergy House - Alfriston

The present house contains a small museum and exhibition. The cottage is surrounded by a small but delightful garden.

Open daily except Tuesdays and Fridays, 1000-1700 from April-October. Entrance: adult: £2.60, child £1.30.

Access via the village centre. Follow signposts. Parking nearby, but not adjacent to the cottage.

Batemans (NT)

This 17th century iron-master's mansion at Burwash was purchased by the famous 20th century writer, Rudyard Kipling, in 1902 following his move from Rottingdean. Here he wrote some of his Sussex masterpieces, including Puck of Pook's Hill. It is now in the care of the National Trust.

The exterior of the house with its distinctive tall chimneys is Jacobean, but inside it shows the stamp of Kipling's India, being much as the author left it during his lifetime. The book-lined study is especially evocative.

There are beautiful gardens, which contain a small stream and watermill. Visitors may also see Kipling's much-loved Rolls-Royce motorcar.

There is a licensed tea-room. Car park. Open daily, except Thursdays and Fridays, April-November 1100-1700.

Entrance: adult £5, child £2.50, family £12.50.

Access via the A265 between Heathfield and Etchingham. Bateman's lies on a lane just off the main road west of the village.

Brighton Pavilion

This brilliant piece of royal eccentricity was built during the period 1815 to 1823 at the behest of George, the Prince of Wales, and later King George IV. The property designed by the famous 19th century architect, John Nash, was built as a seaside retreat within easy travelling distance of London.

The extravagant exterior with its onion shapes and minarets is basically Indian in style, whilst inside the lavish décor is essentially Chinese. Of particular note are the Banqueting Room with its massive table laden with a silver-gilt dinner-service, and the Music Room, with its rich hangings and organ, on which George Frederick Handel is believed to have played.

Royal Pavilion, Brighton

The Pavilion is situated along the Old Steine near the Palace Pier.

Open daily 1000-1800 (1700 October-May). Entrance: adult £4.90, child £3, concessions £3. Local residents £2/free.

Charleston Farmhouse

The most striking feature of this interesting house is the interior decoration. Practically every surface in the house has been painted or decorated in some way! For many years the house was the property of the artists Duncan Grant and Vanessa and Clive Bell, leading members of the so-called 'Bloomsbury Set'. Vivid examples of their work are to be found in the wall-paintings in nearby Berwick church (see Churches). Vanessa Bell was the sister of Virginia Woolf, who discovered the farmhouse in 1916. The rather unconventional household attracted a range of artists and others, including Maynard Keynes, Benjamin Britten and Lytton Strachey.

The small and informal gardens developed by the owners are still very attractive. Since Duncan Grant's death in 1978 the property has been owned by the Charleston Trust, which every year holds a literary and art festival over the last bank holiday weekend in May.

Open April to October, Wednesday-Sunday (and Bank Holiday Mondays), 1400-1700.

Admission: adult £5.50, child £4.00, concessions £4.00 (Wed and Thurs only). Shop, exhibition Gallery and Tea room.

Charleston is signposted off the A27 between Lewes and Polegate.

Firle Place

Originally Tudor, but much altered in the 18th century, Firle has been the family seat of the Gage family for 500 years. The house contains a fine collection of Old Masters together with a unique collection of Sevres pottery. The fine tomb of Sir John Gage, who built Firle, is located in the parish church of St Peter (see Churches) alongside his wife.

Set in gently rolling parkland near Lewes, the house is reached by a long drive. Ample car parking. Elegant tearoom and restaurant. Open May-September, Wednesday-Thursday and Sunday, 1400-1700. Guided tours.

Admission: adult £4.50, child £2, concessions £4.

Firle lies just south of the A27 to the east of Lewes.

Glynde Place

Glynde Place, not to be confused with the nearby Glyndebourne Opera house, is an elegant Elizabethan manor house built of flint and Normandy stone in 1569. Its first owner was one Wm Morley, a wealthy landowner from Hertfordshire.

In the 18th century, the house was extended and embellished and now contains a fine collection of paintings, furniture and ceramics. The collection includes several Old Masters, such as Canaletto, Guardi and Sir Peter Lely. There is also a unique sketch by Rubens painted on wood of a design for the ceiling of Whitehall Palace for King James I.

In the 17th century one previous owner, Harbert Morley, played an important role for the Parliamentarians in the English Civil War. He was one of the judges at the trial of Charles I, but refused to sign the death warrant. This enabled him to obtain a pardon from Charles II when he was returned to power in 1660. An exhibition of Civil War memorabilia is on display for visitors.

The present occupants of the house are Viscount and Viscountess Hampden.

Open Sundays & Bank Holidays from May-September in the afternoon, and on Wednesday and Thursday afternoons during July and August. Entrance: adult £4, child £2.

Northiam, Great Dixter

The house and gardens at Great Dixter are an authentic combination of English native building and horticulture. The house was built in the mid-15th century, and later restored by the famous architect of English country houses, Sir Edwin Lutyens, in 1910.

The Great Hall is one of the best examples of a timber-framed hall in England. The extension to the building in 1910 included the re-erection of another timber-framed house, brought piece by piece from nearby Benenden under Lutyens' supervision.

The present owner, Christopher Lloyd, has spent his life developing some truly stunning gardens around the property.

Open daily except Monday, 1400-1700 April-October. Admission (House and garden): adult £6, child £1.50; gardens only, adult £4.50, child £1.

Rodmell, Monk's House (NT)

This was the former residence of novelist Virginia Woolf and her writer husband, Leonard, until his death in 1969. The house contains a number of memorabilia of the Woolfs and their literary circle. Virginia Woolf is considered to be a great, innovative novelist, whose ideas such as the 'stream of consciousness' have been taken up by many subsequent authors. Unfortunately, she suffered from chronic depression, and in 1941 drowned herself in the river Ouse not far from the house.

The house is occupied and visiting is restricted. Open Wednesdays and Saturdays 1400-1730, April-October. Admission: adult £2.50, child £1.25, family £6.25.

Rye, Lamb House (NT)

This delightful 18th century house was once the home of the American novelist, Henry James, from 1898-1916, and contains a small exhibition of James's personal effects and an attractive walled garden. James was noted for his pyschological novels and short stories, one of which, *The Turn of the Screw*, became widely known at the turn of the 20th century. Later the house was occupied by the popular writer, E.F.Benson, who died in 1940.

The house is named after its owner, James Lamb, thirteen times mayor of Rye, and is still a private residence, so visiting hours are restricted.

The house is located in West Street. It was given to the National Trust by the widow of Henry James's nephew in 1948 as *'an enduring symbol of the ties that unite the British and American people'*.

Open Wednesday and Saturday 1400-1800, April-Oct. Admission: adult £2.50, child £1.25.

Scotney Castle Garden (NT)

These delightful gardens, owned and managed by the National Trust, lie just across the Kent-Sussex border, but are included here for those visiting the eastern part of the county.

There is an intimacy about these gardens that is enhanced by the attractiveness of the remains of the 14th century castle that they share. The walks around the site are especially enjoyable during spring and autumn when the shrubs and trees are at their best. However, it should be noted that some areas of the garden are quite steep.

Open daily end March-end September, except for Mondays and Tuesdays, 1100-1800 weekdays, 1400-1800 weekends.

Admission: adult £4.40, child £2.20, family £11. Free parking. Shop.

Sheffield Park Garden (NT)

The magnificent and extensive landscaped gardens of Sheffield Park are a jewel in the crown of the National Trust. The present layout with its four lakes linked by various waterfalls owes its form to the genius of Lancelot 'Capability' Brown (1715-83). The property is perhaps at its best in the spring or in autumn, but is beautiful at any time of the year. The house is not open to visitors. Open daily 1030-1800 (excepting Mondays) from 1st March-30 October. Weekends only November-February, closing at 1600. Entrance: adult £4.50, child £2.25, family £11.25. Access via A275 north of junction with A272, just past the Bluebell steam railway station.

Standen (NT)

This showpiece Victorian family house is decorated throughout with William Morris designs and other fine examples of the Arts and Crafts Movement. There are pre-Raphaelite paintings by Burne-Jones, Maddox Brown and others. There are extensive views over the Sussex Weald from the garden terraces.

The house is open March to November daily except Mondays and Tuesdays from 1230-1630. Admission: adult £5, family £12.50. Garden only £3.

Access from the B2110 between Turners Hill and East Grinstead.

Ticehurst, Pashley Manor Gardens

The manor house, dating from the mid-16th century is a fine example of a Tudor timber-framed mansion with 18th century additions. The house, set in parkland, is a family home, but the eight acres of formal gardens are open to the public. There are ponds, waterfalls and a moat, all combining to make this a most attractive spot.

Open April - September, Tuesday, Wednesday, Thursday and Saturday, 1100-1700. Teas and lunches available.

Admission: adult £5, child £4.50, concessions £4.50.

Access via B2099 west of A21 just north of Hurst Green on the Hastings road.

Wakehurst Place

These exciting gardens are maintained by the Royal Botanic Gardens at Kew. They contain a huge variety of trees, shrubs and plants from all over the world all set in and around a steep-sided valley leading down to a small lake with an associated nature reserve.

Wakehurst Place

The Japanese water-garden is just one of several attractive ornamental features at Wakehurst. Such is the range of shrubs and plants on display that the site is worth visiting at almost any time of the year. Not surprisingly, this is the most visited attraction in West Sussex year after year.

A recent major addition to the complex is the Millennium Seed Bank, opened by Prince Charles in 2000. The Bank contains millions of seeds from all over the world, which are stored at 20 degrees Celsius to preserve them against extinction. There is a vivid virtual reality guide to the cold stores.

The Elizabethan house on the site is also open to visitors, and there is a shop and self-service restaurant.

Open daily from 1000-1700. Entrance: adults £5, child £3.50, concessions £3.50, family ticket £13. Free to National Trust members.

Access via B2028 via Ardingly about five miles north of Haywards Heath.

Nature Reserves and Beauty Spots

Ashdown Forest - Old Lodge Nature Reserve

Beachy Head

Bentley Wildfowl Centre

Bewl Water

Birling Gap

Cuckmere Haven/ Seven Sisters

Lewes - Malling Down Nature Reserve

Lullington Heath National Nature Reserve

Pett Pools Nature Reserve

Rye Harbour Nature Reserve

East Sussex is blessed with some stunning cliff-top views, and the contrasting beauty of the smooth, treeless hilltops of the Downs and the varied contours of the richly-wooded Weald. Many areas of the Downs and the Weald are designated areas of outstanding natural beauty, and contain important nature reserves established to protect rare plants and wildlife. Several of these are managed by the Sussex Wildlife Trust, which also has a large educational programme in the area. There are also coastal reserves that serve to protect seabirds and waterfowl along what is one of the most populated coastlines in the whole of Britain. The countryside environment is sustained by important partnerships between farmers, landowners and conservation bodies. Without adequate grazing and wildlife management schemes the Downs would lose much of their flora and fauna. We have selected just a few of the locations that are typical of the East Sussex countryside, and well worth seeing by those interested in the history and culture of the county in its natural setting.

Ashdown Forest - Old Lodge Nature Reserve
This heathland nature reserve is managed by the Sussex Wildlife Trust. Such heathland is the result of centuries of animal grazing on the light, sandy soil. The Trust is encouraging grazing by sheep, cattle and Exmoor ponies in order to maintain the habitat of rare heathland plants.

The forest itself disappeared several centuries ago when the weald was at the centre of the glass and iron-making industry and trees were needed to produce charcoal to charge the foundries. Wealden oak was also highly-prized by the ship-builders of the Cinque Ports and the Thames. The Ashdown forest maintained more than the usual amount of common land both in medieval times and later. The result today is the extensive open area which can be enjoyed by all.

Look out for Stonechats, Redstarts and Nightjars, which breed on the reserve.

Access from car park just north of the junction of the B2026 and the B2188. The B2026 leads off the A22 north of Maresfield.

Beachy Head
This wonderful stretch of English coastline, part of the South Downs Way, loses nothing by being included in almost every South Coast itinerary. The majestic height and line of these magnificent chalk cliffs rising to over 500 feet never cease to enthral both locals and visitors alike. As the cliffs are not fenced off, it is important not to walk too close to the edge. It is not without reason that this spot is one of the prime places for suicides in the area.

Objects of interest here include the Beachy Head lighthouse with its distinctive red and white stripes at the base of the cliffs, and the old Belle Tout lighthouse standing high on the cliff-top midway between the Head and Birling Gap. The latter was built in 1825, and served until 1902, when it was superseded by the present lighthouse. In March 1999, in a spectacular, though slow-moving, engineering feat, it was lifted up bodily and moved 17 metres (50 feet) inland to prevent its collapse into the sea.

There is a Beachy Head Countryside Centre with displays (admission free), and a restaurant opposite the coastguard station. Reasonable off-road parking.

The cliffs are best approached via the A259 at East Dean, or via the B2103 from Eastbourne.

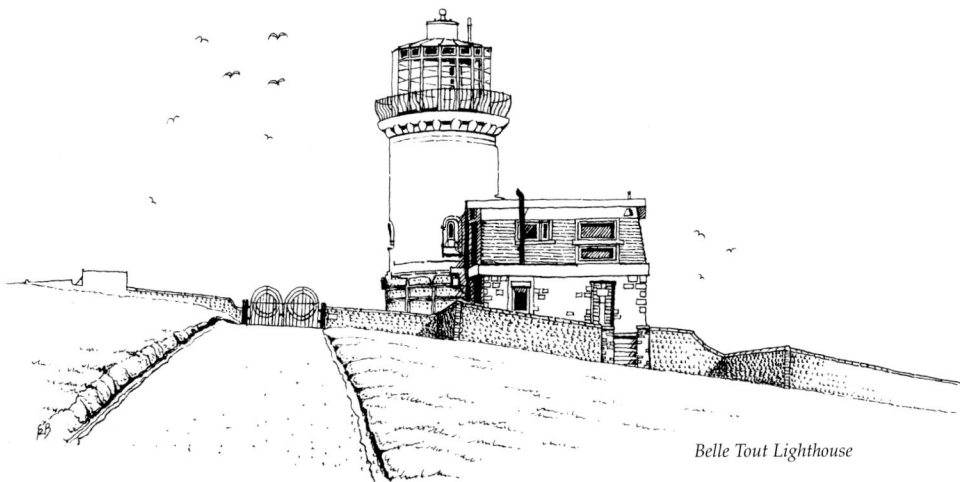

Belle Tout Lighthouse

Bentley Wildfowl Centre

The Bentley collection of wildfowl was started by Gerald Askew in the 1960's. It is now the largest private collection in Britain with more than 1000 birds representing some 115 different species of waterfowl.

The reserve is less rugged than those at Arundel or Pagham (in West Sussex), but it always manages to be more than an ornamental place.

In addition to the wildfowl reserve, the visitor is also able to enjoy other features of the complex. There is a museum of modern motor-car history, formal gardens, a woodland trail, and a stately home all of which may be visited for the same fee.

There is a refreshment room and shop. Ample parking. Open daily March-October, 1030-1630 (1700 July/August). House opens 1200. During winter open weekends only 1030-1600 (House closed).

Admission: adult £4.80, child £3, family £14.50, concessions £3.80.

Access via the A26 between Lewes and Uckfield and then follow signposts.

Bewl Water

This large reservoir was completed in 1976 to supply water to the North Kent area. With a circumference of some 15 miles, it is now the largest lake in the south of England. The irregular outline of the reservoir enabled the owners to provide for boating and other water-sports, as well as developing a quiet nature reserve for birdwatchers and walkers. Boat trips available.

Visitor Centre, nature trails and picnic areas available. Open daily all year 0900-sunset. Admission free.

Bewl lies close to Lamberhurst, Wadhurst and Ticehurst. Best approached off A21 at Lamberhurst along B2100.

Birling Gap

Much of what has been said about Beachy Head applies to this neighbouring stretch of coast. Of particular interest here are the effects of the erosion of the cliffs due to rain, wind and waves. The coastguard cottages which once stood some way from the cliff-top are now practically falling into the sea. Access to the beach is by means of a stairway that can be winched back towards the cliff to counter the effects of the erosion.

Refreshments and toilet facilities available. Car park. Access is simplest south from the A259 at East Dean.

Cuckmere Haven/ Seven Sisters

The point where the river Cuckmere flows through the Downs into the English Channel provides one of the most striking examples of an oxbow lake that one could ever wish to see! Viewed from the high ground to the east of the water-meadows the river snakes backwards and forwards until almost at the shore-line. Sheep are grazed here, accompanied for most of the year by large flocks of Canada geese.

The area forms the central feature of the Seven Sisters Country Park.

Access off the A259 east of Seaford, either at the Golden Galleon public house, or a little further on at the Butterfly Centre. Parking may be difficult at peak times. Entry free.

Lewes, Malling Down Nature Reserve

Overlooking the eastern outskirts of Lewes lies Malling Down. The chalk downland supports a wide variety of attractive plants, such as the Common Spotted Orchid, Small Scabious and the Rock Rose. Rare chalkland butterflies, such as the Adonis Blue breed here, as well as Glow-worms that light up the reserve on warm summer nights.

The terrain is rather hilly and uneven, and a tour of the whole site takes up to about 3 hours. Access for drivers is best from the B2192 Lewes-Ringmer road, where there is a lay-by on the right-hand side.

For walkers the site can be accessed from the Wheatsheaf Gardens in Malling Street on the A26 to Tunbridge Wells.

Lullington Heath National Nature Reserve

This nature reserve comprises the largest area of chalk heathland in the South. This rare habitat is produced where there is an acidic layer of topsoil on the chalk. Visitors can see heather, rare orchids and other plants, as well as a range of butterflies native to the chalk downland. The site covers some 177 acres of heathland and some associated woodland. Resident birds include kestrels and sparrow-hawks, whilst visitors include the nightingale and a variety of warblers. The site is managed by English Nature.

The reserve lies between Litlington and Jevington on the downland west of Eastbourne. Access by signed footpaths.

Pett Pools Nature Reserve

About halfway between Hastings and Rye lie the Pett Pools, dug out in the 1940's to provide material for local sea defences. There are four separate pools, two fairly shallow and two quite deep. In July each year the water levels in Pool 1 are reduced to uncover mudflats for wading birds, such as Redshank, Grey Plover and Black-tailed Godwit. Breeding birds include the rare Bearded Tit.

The reserve itself is closed to the public, but there is a clear viewing point from the beach road between Fairlight and Winchelsea. Access from A259 at Ore east of Hastings in direction of Fairlight.

Rye Harbour Nature Reserve

This substantial nature reserve is noted above all for its bird life, especially its breeding colonies of Little, Common and Sandwich Terns and other ground nesting birds, such as Ringed Plover, Lapwing and Wheatear. Rye's location makes it an important staging post for migratory birds, as well as providing ample feeding grounds for winter visitors. More than 280 different species have been recorded on the reserve.

The reserve is also interesting because of its rare shingle vegetation with masses of Sea Kale, Yellow Horned Poppy and Sea Pea to be seen in May and June. The varied nature of the site, which includes freshwater pools and ditches as well as saltmarsh, attracts more than 400 species of flowering plants and more than 2000 species of invertebrates.

For the historian, there is the chance to see a Martello Tower (near the car park) and Camber Castle, a rare example of a fort built by Henry VIII (see Castles).

Access via A259 on eastern approach to Rye (clearly signposted). Follow road past industrial area to car park about one mile from main road.

Museums

Battle Museum

Bexhill Museum

Ditchling Museum

Eastbourne, Redoubt Fortress

Eastbourne, Museum of Shops

Eastbourne, RNLI Museum

Hastings, White Rock

Hastings, Shipwreck Heritage Centre

Hastings, Smugglers Adventure

Herstmonceux, Science Centre

Hove, British Engineerium

Lewes, Anne of Cleves House

Lewes, Barbican Museum

Newhaven Fort

Rottingdean Museum

Rye Heritage Centre

Rye Museum (see Castles)

Seaford, Martello Tower

East Sussex has a wide range of museums aimed at demonstrating the long and varied history of the area. Some focus on prehistoric and medieval times, others on the Tudor period up to Napoleonic times, and a few concentrate on the twentieth century. Most of the museums are themselves sited in historic locations - castles, defensive towers, merchants' houses and an engineering works, to name just a few. Increasingly, museums are using modern technology to present their exhibits, including life-size models, realistic soundtracks and audio-visual programmes. Entry fees are usually modest, and some museums are free. Some are managed by voluntary groups, others by local authorities or commercial organisations. All provide vivid opportunities for visitors to sense what life was like for those living in earlier times.

Battle Museum

This small museum is situated in the Memorial Hall in the High Street, a short distance from the famous abbey (see under Churches and Priories).

As well as displays relating to the Battle of Hastings (1066) and the Bayeux Tapestry, there are items about various aspects of the history of this ancient town, including the development of the local gunpowder industry.

Open daily April-October, 1030-1630 (1400-1700 Suns).

Admission: adult £1, child £0.20.

Bexhill Museum

The local museum contains several interesting displays relating to its history, mainly from the 18th century onwards. Of particular note is the scale model of the De La Warr Pavilion, the art deco building that caused such controversy when it was opened in 1935. Nevertheless, such worthies as Sir George Bernard Shaw and Sir Adrian Boult spoke in its favour as a centre for the arts in the area.

There are memorabilia of John Logie Baird, the radio pioneer, who lived in Bexhill before his death in 1946. There is also a display relating to the Kings German Legion (KGL), the Hanoverian troops who were billeted in the town during the Napoleonic Wars.

For those interested in World War II, there is a display of Battle Of Britain photographs, and other RAF artefacts, including parts of a Spitfire VB, which crashed into the sea off the town in September 1941. There is also a chair used by Air Marshal Lord Dowding in his retirement.

Other displays relate to the early history of the area and to its wildlife.

Centurion tank (Mk. III)

Open Tuesday-Friday 1000-1700, weekends and Bank Holidays 1400-1700, throughout the year (except January, closed).

Entry: adult £1, concessions £0.50, children free. Located in Egerton Road, near seafront Clock Tower.

Ditchling Museum

Housed in the former Victorian village school, this little museum has much to offer. In addition to the displays of rural life in the village, the museum also contains a special gallery dedicated to the life and times of Eric Gill and the other artists and craftsmen who joined him in the early 20th century, part of the Arts and Crafts Movement.

Open April-October daily except Mondays 1030-1700 (1400-1700 Sundays).

Admission: adult £2.50, child £0.50p, concessions £1.50. Shop and refreshments.

The museum is located in Church Lane to the north of the village crossroads. Access via the A23 at Pyecombe taking the A273 and then B2112.

Eastbourne, Redoubt Fortress

Based in a strongpoint, built between 1804-1810 to defend Britain's shores against possible invasion by Napoleon Bonaparte, this is the largest museum of military history in the south-east of England. Outside the museum is a Centurion tank (Mk. III), which last saw action during the Battle of the Imjin River in the Korean War in 1951, when the 1st Bn the Gloucester Regiment fought a famous rearguard action against massive Chinese forces. The Redoubt contains numerous memorabilia of World War II, when the fortress served as an anti-aircraft battery under the Canadians. There are also displays relating to the Royal Sussex Regiment and other military subjects over the past 300 years. There is even a Merlin engine rescued from a Spitfire that crashed at Wilmington during the Battle of Britain.

Open daily 1000-1730 April-November.

Admission: adult £2.20, child £1.10, concessions £1.10, family ticket £5.90.

The fortress is located on the seafront in the Royal Parade.

Eastbourne, Museum of Shops

For those interested in shopping, this fascinating museum is a must. The examples on display show how shops looked like in the days before supermarkets. The displays include a grocer's, an ironmonger's, a chemist's and a draper's shop to name just a few. There is also a seafarer's inn and a wartime kitchen from the Second World War.

The museum is sub-titled 'How we lived Then', and is situated in an 1850 town house in the centre of the town.

Open daily 1000-1730, April-October.

Admission: adult £3, child £2, concessions £2.50.

Eastbourne, RNLI Museum

Every major seaside resort owes a debt to the lifeboatmen who have turned out to help sailors and swimmers in distress. The Eastbourne lifeboat station has seen more than a fair share of action in its 150 years of history. This seafront museum tells the story of these years in photographs and local memorabilia.

Located at the Wish Tower in King Edward's Parade. Open daily Easter to January.

Admission free.

Hastings, Shipwreck Heritage Centre

This fascinating museum is devoted entirely to shipwrecks, including both ships and their cargoes. Of particular interest are the remains of a Roman ship from the 2nd century, the complete hull of a 15th century sailing barge rescued from the Thames, and the last Rye barge, the Primrose, built in the 1890's. There are many artefacts rescued from ships that went down off the Hastings coast,

Open daily April-October 1030-1700, reduced opening hours during the winter. Free admission, but donations welcome. Guided tours £1.

Nearby are the Hastings Lifeboat Station and Visitor Centre, and the Fishermen's Museum, which are open all year.

Hastings, Smugglers Adventure

The caves have been transformed by modern technology to re-create the time when smuggling was an important albeit illegal activity in the Hastings area. The lighting and sounds are dramatic, adding to the atmosphere created by life-size figures, all set in the labyrinth of caves and passages that form St Clement's Caves.

The original caves began as fissures in the rocks, but were exploited for their sandstone, which was used in glassmaking as well as for strewing on floors. It is known that in 1797 the caves were enlarged to make way for a military hospital for the Duke of Wellington's troops in the fighting against Napoleon. During World War II the caves were used as a large air-raid shelter, complete with school and medical centre.

The exhibition is open daily all year. Summer 1000-1730, winter 1000-1630.

Admission: adult £5.25, child £3.40, concessions £4.25, family £14.75. Guide-books and notes available in French.

Access to the entrance to the caves is by a number of steep narrow steps leading to the top of West Hill.

Hastings, White Rock

The White Rock Theatre overlooking the seafront is home to the Hastings Embroidery commissioned in 1966 to commemorate the 900th anniversary of the Battle of Hastings. This famous piece of needlework captures some 81 different events in British history since the time of the Conquest. The artwork is striking.

Admission: adult £2, child and concessions £1.00. Open all year.

Herstmonceux, Science Centre

The centre is based on the site of the former Greenwich Observatory, which was located at Herstmonceux for more than 30 years. Now the green domes that sheltered the massive telescopes of the Observatory are in service as a museum of science and discovery. There are daily telescope tours and a 'hands-on' science centre with more than 80 exhibits.

Open to the public daily 1000-1800 April-October, and for pre-booked visits during the winter.

Admission: adult £4.50, child £3.30, concessions £3.30, family ticket £13.

Access via A271 Hailsham-Pevensey road at signpost to the east of Herstmonceux village.

Hove, British Engineerium

Housed in a former Victorian water-pumping station, this museum contains a unique collection of engineering exhibits. These range from huge steam-driven beam engines, traction engines, steam boats, vintage motor cycles and old fire engines to a jet engine designed by Sir Frank Whittle. There are numerous working models and other exhibits, including several hands-on items.

Open daily all year 1000-1700.

Admission: adult £4, child £3, concessions £3, family ticket £12.

The Engineerium lies off Nevill Road, Hove, just past the Greyhound Stadium.

Lewes, Anne of Cleves House

This elegant timber-framed house, now in the care of the Sussex Archaelogical Society, was given to Anne of Cleves as part of her divorce settlement by Henry VIII. The house now contains a variety of displays and artefacts relating to the social life of the county town of Lewes from medieval times. Of particular interest are the old kitchen, the main chamber and the display of Sussex iron-making.

Anne of Cleves House

There are also several stone artefacts from the ruins of the former Lewes Priory, and a replica of the tombstone of Gundrada, wife of William de Warenne, who founded both castle and priory. The original tombstone now lies in Southover Church a short distance away.

Open daily mid-February to November, 1000-1700 (Sundays 1200-1700). Limited opening during winter.

Admission: adult £2.60, child £1.30, concessions £2.40. Combined tickets for castle and Barbican Museum also available.

Lewes, Barbican Museum

The Barbican museum is set in a town house adjacent to the substantial remains of the 14th century barbican of Lewes castle. There are displays of local life from Norman times up to the present, a working model of the town, and other displays relating to the local landscape and its heritage.

Entrance to the Museum includes entrance to the castle - a magnificent sight in its own right (see under Castles).

Open daily 1000-1730 (Sunday opening 1100). Castle closes at dusk in winter.

Admission: adult £4, child £2, concessions £3.50. Combined tickets for Anne of Cleves House available.

Newhaven Fort

For details of this museum of military history please see under Castles.

Rottingdean, The Grange Art Gallery & Museum

The highlight of this little museum set in an elegant Georgian property is the display relating to the life of Rudyard Kipling, who lived in a neighbouring house overlooking the village pond. There is also an interesting collection of children's toys since Victorian times. The gallery displays art by talented local artists. The public library on the ground floor has a good collection of Kipling books.

Open daily 1000-1600, except Wednesday (closed) and Sunday (1400-1600).

Admission free.

Rye Museum

This museum is in two parts, one centred on the Ypres Tower (see under Castles), and the other in East Street. The majority of exhibits are in the latter, which includes Rye's old fire engine used between 1745 and 1865, and the sanctuary knocker from St Mary's church. There are various memorabilia relating to the Cinque Ports, and a model of the harbour as it was in earlier times. There is a display of Victorian parlour games and toys, and a large collection of Rye pottery since the 1840's. One item of farming history is the silver tankard presented in 1852 for the Best Fat Cow in Sussex or Kent!

The East Street site is open April-October, weekdays only 1400-1700.

Tower open daily April-October (except Tuesday/ Wednesday).

Admission (both sites): adult £2.90, child £1.50, concessions £2, family ticket £5.90. One site only: adult £1.90, child £1, concessions £1.50, family £4.50.

Both sites are well sign-posted in Rye town centre, which is situated at the eastern boundary of the county off the A259.

Rye Heritage Centre

The centre contains a theatre holding 50 people where a scale model of the ancient Cinque Port of Rye is brought to life by a sound and light display, telling the story of the town from its earliest days. Foreign language commentaries are available in French, German and Spanish. Entry to the display includes a free visit to an exhibition of historical artefacts and pictures relating to the town.

Admission: adult £2, child £1, concessions £1.50. Open daily all year.

The centre is located in the same building as the Tourist Information Office on Strand Quay.

Seaford, Martello Tower

This little museum of local life is housed in a former Martello tower. Between 1805 and 1812 more than 70 such towers were built to defend the south coast against invasion by Napoleon. The name derives from a similar tower at Mortella Point in Corsica, which in an earlier conflict (1794) had provided stout resistance to British forces. Each tower was designed to deflect cannon fire by providing thick, rounded walls and skirting. They were usually mounted by a 24 pounder cannon, although the one here is a 32 pounder. Only a few Martello towers survive today, mostly along the Sussex coast.

The museum contains a range of displays of local folk history, including a general store, a Victorian schoolroom, and a collection of domestic and office equipment. There is a working model of Seaford railway station as it was in 1926, and there are memorabilia from the Second World War.

The museum is operated by volunteers, and opening hours are therefore limited to Sundays and Bank Holidays during the year (1100-1630) and Wednesdays during the summer months (1430-1630).

Admission: adult £1, child £0.50.

Martello Tower

Steam Railways

Bluebell Railway

Kent & East Sussex Railway

Lavender Line

East Sussex is fortunate to have three stretches of line dedicated to steam working. All run on what were once important branch lines until the cutbacks of the 1950's. All the railways are operated by voluntary organisations, which depend on active participation by their keenest members as well as by the financial support that all members give. All three services charge modest fares for their journeys, which vary in length from about two to twelve miles for a return trip. Most of the companies allow fare-paying visitors to visit their engine sheds. All provide buffet facilities and a shop for memorabilia.

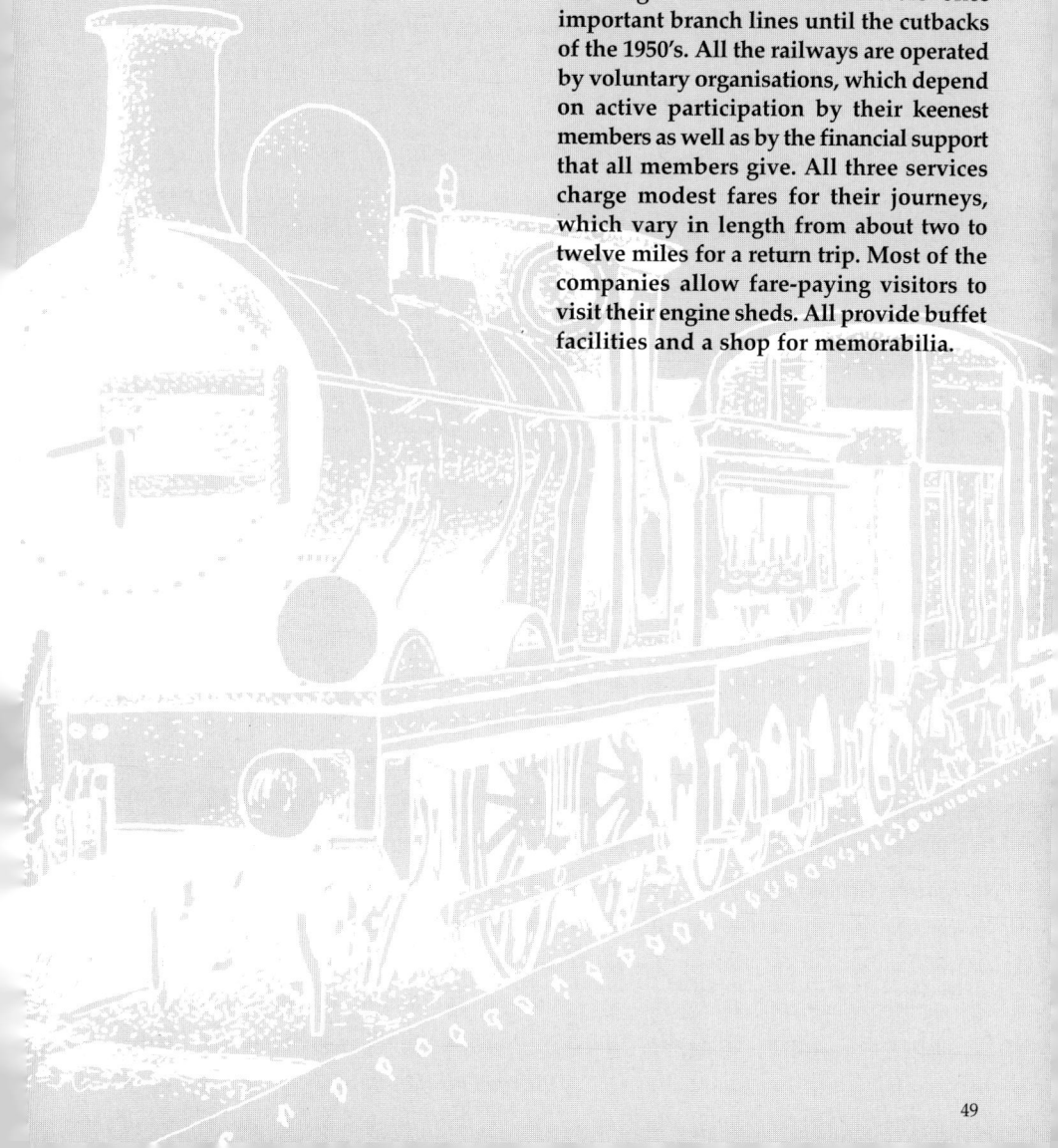

Bluebell Railway

The Bluebell Line operates an 18 mile return journey between Sheffield Park and Kingscote. The trains, stations, locomotive sheds and other facilities are all of a highly authentic and professional standard. The Line has succeeded in raising hundreds of thousands of pounds towards its refurbishment and eventual link-up to the main line at East Grinstead.

There are various steam and diesel locomotives on display in the engine sheds at Sheffield Park. The collection has grown to over 30 steam locomotives and more than a 100 carriages and other rolling stock.

At weekends it is possible to book dinner (Saturday) or lunch (Sunday) on a restored Pullman car formerly used on the Golden Arrow service to Paris (Tel 01825-722008). There is a station buffet/restaurant and gift shop.

The service operates at weekends throughout the year, and daily from Easter to end September. Fares: adult £7.80, child £ 3.90, senior citizens £6.20.

The **Greenwich Meridian line** passes close by Sheffield Park station. Access via the A275 north of the A272 between Haywards Heath and Maresfield.

Kent & East Sussex Railway

In the millennium year 2000, a £2m extension to the railway saw Tenterden in Kent linked directly to Bodiam (East Sussex) for the first time in 46 years. The Kent & East Sussex Railway is now the longest steam railway in the South-East of England, covering some 10½ miles of beautiful Wealden countryside.

The line owns twelve steam locomotives from Britain, America and Norway. The passenger carriages date from Victorian times up to the 1950's, when the line was axed as part of a national plan to reduce unprofitable rural services. There are stations at Tenterden, where there is also a railway museum, Northiam and Bodiam. The first two have free car parks, but Bodiam Station does not have any parking.

The timetable operates throughout the year at weekends, and daily from April to September. Fares between Tenterden and Bodiam range from £7.50 adult, £3.75 child and £20 for a family ticket.

Tenterden and Northiam stations are both located on the A28 between Ashford and Hastings. Bodiam is best reached via the A21 between Hastings and Hurst Green. Follow signs.

Lavender Line

This is the smallest of the three railways in the county. It derives its name from Lavender & Sons, the family of coal merchants who operated out of Isfield station. The original line, dating from 1858, ran between Uckfield and Lewes. Now the service begins and ends at Isfield, where the company's locomotives are stored and repaired.

The line covers about a mile and a return journey lasts about 20 minutes. There are several interesting exhibits, ranging from old steam locomotives to slot machines and old timetables.

Buffet facilities. Ample parking.
Fares: adult £3.80, child £2, concessions £3. Site only: £1/ 0.50p

Access via A26 between Lewes and Uckfield at signpost for Isfield.

Other Visits

Clayton, Jack and Jill Windmills

Clayton, The Chattri Monument

Crowborough, Conan Doyle Statue

Pooh Corner

There are a few places of interest to visitors that do not fall into any of the earlier categories in this guide. Windmills are a strong feature of the Sussex landscape, so it is appropriate to include the two mills at Clayton, since not only are they standing side by side, but also they enable visitors to see two different types of windmill at once. The Chattri monument at Clayton set in the heart of the Downs is a reminder of Indian troops who left their native land to fight on Britain's side during World War I. A recent monument is the statue in honour of Sir Arthur Conan Doyle, who lived in Crowborough for many years. Finally, on a lighter note, we remember the literary heritage of A.A.Milne by including the House at Pooh Corner.

Clayton - Jack and Jill Windmills

Windmills are still well in evidence throughout the Sussex Downs, where their prominent positions ensure their visibility for miles. These two windmills are sited on the borders of East and West Sussex, overlooking the village of Clayton.

The white mill nicknamed Jill, is a post mill built in Brighton in 1820 and moved to Clayton in 1852. Restored to full working condition more than a decade ago, it is open to the public on Sunday and Bank Holiday afternoons during the summer months. The black mill, known as Jack, is a tower mill built in 1866. It is currently a private residence and is not open to the public. Access is via the A273 east of the A23 at Pyecombe north of Brighton.

Clayton - The Chattri Monument

This monument was erected in 1921 to commemorate the thousands of Indian troops (Hindus and Sikhs) who died in Britain's service during the First World War, many of them at the military hospital set up in Brighton's Royal Pavilion. The troops had been stationed in the Brighton area and given much of their military training in the Downs overlooking the town. The site above Patcham was therefore an appropriate choice. The octagonal domed monument with its 29^{ft} pillars is made of white Sicilian marble.

The monument is approached on foot from the Sussex Border path between Patcham and Clayton.

Crowborough - Conan Doyle Statue

This life-sized bronze statue to the memory of world famous author, Sir Arthur Conan Doyle, was unveiled in April 2001. Surprisingly, it is the only statue of Conan Doyle in the world, whereas there are several dedicated to the memory of Doyle's famous creation, Sherlock Holmes. The author lived in Crowborough for more than twenty years between 1907 and his death in 1930.

The monument was commissioned by the Town Council, and executed by the sculptor, David Cornell. It stands at the crossroads in the centre of the town on the A26 to Tunbridge Wells.

Pooh Corner (A.A.Milne)

The so-called House at Pooh Corner is a delightful 300 year-old cottage, now a shop of Milne memorabilia. The cottage is located on the southern approach to Hartfield just past the junction of the B2110 and B2026. For directions to the nearby Pooh Sticks bridge it is best to ask at the shop, where a special map is available. Shop open 0900-1700 Monday-Saturday, 1100-1700 Sunday.

Long-distance paths

The Cuckoo Trail

South Downs Way

Sussex Border Path

1066 Country Walk

Vanguard Way

Weald Way

For keen walkers, cyclists and horse-riders, we have included brief details of some of the principal long-distance paths which are open all year round. All of these routes are open to walkers, and most are open to cyclists and horse-riders as well. Most routes have their own specialist guides obtainable from bookshops and tourist information centres. Sign-posting and way-marking are generally of a high standard in the county, so routes are easy to follow. Where walks are considered to be more challenging, this has been indicated. Several of the routes pass by or near places mentioned earlier in this guide. Observance of the Country Code is especially important in this section since so many of the routes pass through farms and private estates.

The Cuckoo Trail

The Cuckoo trail follows the former railway line from Polegate through Hailsham and Horam to Heathfield, a distance of about 11 miles. The trail is open to cyclists and walkers, although some stretches are also open to horse-riders. Clearly sign-posted at key locations, such as Hailsham. There is a cycle centre at the former station at Horam. Being on a former railway line means that the path is very flat and therefore easy to negotiate.

South Downs Way

One of the major downland footpaths in the south of England, the 100 mile long South Downs Way from Winchester to Eastbourne enters East Sussex at Devil's Dyke just north of Brighton and continues onto the coast. It is open to walkers, cyclists and horse-riders along the entire route. The path is suitable for a wide range of walkers.

The bridle-way passes by Jack and Jill windmills at Clayton, and crosses Ditchling Beacon before dropping down to the A27 between Falmer and Lewes. The path continues past Kingston and down towards Rodmell, close to Monk's House, and crosses the river Ouse at Southease. It continues past Firle and Berwick before entering Alfriston.

The route for walkers only continues down to Exceat, Seven Sisters and Beachy Head before ending at Eastbourne. There is an alternative route via Jevington at this point for cyclists and horse-riders.

The entire East Sussex section passes many of the places mentioned earlier in this guide.

Sussex Border Path

This 150 mile path starts at Emsworth in Hampshire and follows the borders around East and West Sussex and the neighbouring counties of Surrey and Kent. In the East Sussex area the path resumes its route from the west near East Grinstead and meanders across the northern parts of the county until reaching its destination at Rye. The path is fairly challenging, and is for walkers only.

A separate guidebook (£4) is available from the Ramblers Association (Tel. 01273-883306).

1066 Country Walk

As its title implies, this path takes the visitor along sites associated with the battle of Hastings in 1066. Starting in the east at Rye, the path passes through Winchelsea, past Icklesham and Westfield on the way to Battle. From there the route follows a south-westerly direction to its destination at Pevensey, passing close to Herstmonceux on the way. The total distance covered is about 31 miles, and includes several places mentioned in this guide. For walkers only.

Vanguard Way

This path follows a generally north-south route, commencing east of East Grinstead near Hammerwood Park, and dropping down towards Forest Row before crossing the Ashdown Forest and reaching Buxted. Here the route crosses the A272 and continues towards the village of Blackboys, where it drops southwards towards Chiddingly, crossing the A22 near Golden Cross. The path continues southwards past Chalvington to cross the A27 near Berwick en route to Alfriston and Seven Sisters before striking out along the coast towards Seaford and Newhaven, its final destination. The path is for walkers only and is fairly challenging.

Weald Way

Commencing from the south at Eastbourne, this path takes the walker across the Downs to Jevington and past the Long Man at Wilmington. Crossing the

A27 west of Wilmington, the route continues northwards along the Cuckmere river towards Michelham and Hellingly. The path crosses the Vanguard Way at Chiddingly and continues to East Hoathly and the outskirts of Uckfield before striking north across the Ashdown Forest. The path passes through Duddleswell and on towards Hartfield, passing near Pooh Corner and Pooh Sticks bridge. The path leaves the county just to the west of Groombridge on its way to its destination at Gravesend in Kent.

Note: The Ordnance Survey Explorer Maps most relevant to East Sussex are No's. 135, 122, 123, and 124. For areas bordering Kent see No's. 136 and 125.

South Downs Way -Jack and Jill Windmills

Glossary for visits to churches

Aisle. This is an extension, or wing, of a nave (see below) separated from the latter by an arcade of columns. Many parish churches have one aisle, some have two and a few have none.

Altar. The table-like structure located at the east end of a typical parish church was the focal point for the sacrifice of the Mass in pre-Reformation times, and may still be used for eucharistic services in the Church of England. Where the original altar stone survives, it can be identified by the consecration crosses carved in each of its corners. Cathedrals and other large churches usually have several altars set in chapels in the aisles or transepts, in addition to the High Altar in the sanctuary.

Apse. In effect this is a semi-circular chancel providing space at the east end of a church, especially during the Saxon period, in which the main altar could be placed.

Breeches Bible. The name given to the English version of the Geneva bible published by Calvinist Protestants in 1560. The odd name is a reference to the translation of fig-leaf as breeches in the story of Adam and Eve (Gen 3.7). There is an example at St. Mary's, Battle.

Chancel. This is the eastern part of a typical parish church in which the main altar, choir and sanctuary would be located. Here the Blessed Sacrament was reserved - the consecrated bread become Body of Christ - used for the communion of the sick as well as for distribution at Mass. In medieval times it was always separated from the nave by a rood-screen (see below). The chancel was often developed after the building of the nave.

Chantry. A chapel or altar set aside for Masses for the dead. Wealthy benefactors in the Middle Ages donated money for prayers to be said for them and their families after their death. The chantry chapels at St. Thomas, Winchelsea, and All Saints, Herstmonceux, are excellent examples.

Choir. Part of the chancel area reserved for the monks or canons in religious communities. It was sited at the western end, and nowadays is still used for parish choirs.

Crucifix. A cross bearing the crucified figure of Jesus Christ.

Early English. See Early Gothic style below.

Font. The stone receptacle used for the baptism of infants into the Christian community. It is usually bowl-shaped and standing on a stone pedestal. Most of the fonts in the churches described in this guide are medieval or earlier.

Fresco. Painting carried out on wet (fresh) plaster - a favoured practice in medieval times, enabling the Gospels and Christian teaching to be illustrated for the worshipper.

Gothic style. In the last quarter of the 12th century and the early part of the 13th century the pointed arch became favoured over the rounded solidity of the Norman (Romanesque) style. New churches built in this style, originating in France, enabled lighter structures to be put in place, and allowed more space for windows. The first examples of this style are known as Early Gothic (or Early English). Later forms were known as Decorated (c.1250-1350) and Perpendicular (1350-1540). The ceilings in Gothic churches were considerably higher than in their Norman equivalent as their curved structures could be supported by a number of columns and associated vaulting.

Host. The consecrated wafer considered by Catholics to be the Body of Christ. The elevation of the host was the highpoint of a medieval Mass.

Knights Hospitaller. Medieval Christian knights of St John of Jerusalem who maintained pilgrim hospices, hospitals and care for lepers. Their Sussex headquarters were at Poling, near Arundel. Hospitallers are recognised by a white Maltese cross on a black background.

Knights Templar. Arising from the Crusades this military order combined both military and monastic features. They amassed considerable wealth during the 13/14th century, but were suppressed by the Pope in 1312 and many of their houses given to the Hospitallers.

Lectern. This is basically a book-rest supported on a pedestal and column, often in the shape of an eagle, the emblem of St John the Evangelist, from which the scripture readings are said. It is sited to the right of the chancel opposite the pulpit.

Mass. The Mass (in Latin) was the central act of worship in English medieval churches until it was abolished during the Protestant Reformation in the second half of the 16th century. Its emphasis was two-fold: first, to re-enact the sacrifice of Christ at Calvary, and second, to bring the 'Real Presence' of Christ into the community through the consecration of bread and wine in the words Jesus used at the Last Supper. Communion, in the sense of receiving the body and blood of Christ in the form of bread and wine distributed towards the end of Mass, was not frequent in the Middle Ages. Most people only received communion once a year at Easter, but wanted the blessing of the sacred elements as they were raised aloft during Mass. The Church of England retained a form of the communion service, commonly known as the Eucharist (thanksgiving). Roman Catholics still celebrate Mass, though in the vernacular.

Mass dial. A sundial usually set on a plaque on the side of a medieval church near the principal entrance in order to indicate the time. There are good examples at Bishopstone and Lindfield parish churches. Clocks were not available on church towers until the 16th Century, and the best example is to be found at St. Mary's, Rye.

Misericord. Usually a carving of a figure or beast on the underside of the hinged seat in a choir row. There are good examples at Etchingham.

Nave. The western and principal section of any parish church. The term 'nave' originates from the Latin for 'ship', since the roof of the nave was built like an inverted ship. The nave was essentially reserved for the people, unlike the chancel, which was the preserve of the clergy and their attendants (or of monks, in cases where the church was shared between the parish and a religious community, as at Etchingham). Most naves have a great West door, used only on great festivals, with a porched South or North entrance providing the usual entry. The unusual two-storey porch at Lindfield is an interesting example.

Neo-classical style. This refers to church monuments installed in the 18th century to the memory of wealthy or notable individuals. They are characterised by the use of Grecian urns and figures carved from marble. Their appearance is often at odds with the rest of the interior of the typical parish church.

Norman period. The period following the Norman Conquest of Anglo- Saxon England in 1066 in which many castles and churches were built. The Norman style in churches is typified by sturdy columns and rounded arches with dog-toothing (zig-zag) designs on them.

Piscina. Stone bowl set into sanctuary wall near the altar to enable washing of sacred vessels. A piscina always drained into the soil outside. There is a good example at St. Andrew's, Alfriston.

Reredos. This is a wooden or stone screen placed directly behind the High Altar. Few medieval examples survive, but the Victorian Gothic revival (see below) ensured that typical subjects would once again grace England's country churches.

Rood-screen. The rood-screen usually separated the nave from the chancel, and comprised a wooden or stone screen surmounted by the 'rood', i.e. a crucifix with the figures of Mary, mother of Christ, and St John, the Evangelist. Some screens contained a rood-loft, enabling access to the rood itself. Most rood-screens were destroyed at the Reformation.

Sanctuary. The area of the chancel around the altar, usually accessed only by clergy and altar-servers. The altar in medieval churches was topped by a secure tabernacle in which the Blessed Sacrament was kept.

Sedilia. Wall-seats provided for priest and deacons celebrating Mass in medieval times. They were set into the south side of the chancel. A good example can be seen at St. Andrew's, Alfriston.

Shrine. This is usually the site of the tomb or relic of a saint. England's most famous shrine for centuries was that of Thomas a Becket, murdered at Canterbury in 1170. The shrine of Our Lady of Walsingham in Norfolk was even earlier (11th century). There, as in West Grinstead today, the shrine is neither tomb nor relic but a statue of the Blessed Virgin with the Child Jesus. Shrines are essentially places of prayer. Few medieval shrines survived the iconoclasm of the Protestant Reformers.

Squint. This refers to a tunnel-shaped opening made in the chancel arch so as to enable a priest at a side chapel to synchronise his celebration of Mass with the principal celebrant at the High Altar. There are interesting examples at All Saints, Mountfield, and St. Anne's, Lewes.

Tie-beam. This was a huge wooden beam used to secure the walls of a nave or a chancel.

Transepts. These are the arms that extend to the south and north of a cruciform (cross-shaped) church, usually between the nave and the chancel. Only larger churches tend to have transepts, as at Fletching and Lindfield.

Victorian Gothic. In the mid-nineteenth century interest was awakened in the restoration of England's parish churches and the building of new churches. Under the influence of architects such as Scott, Pugin and Hansom ancient churches were restored or rebuilt, and new ones constructed. Many of the medieval churches in this guide felt the benefit (or otherwise) of Victorian refurbishment.

Index

Page

Alfriston, Clergy House (NT) — 34
Alfriston, St Andrew's — 18
Ashdown Forest, Old Lodge Nature Reserve — 40
Batemans (NT) — 34
Battle Abbey (EH) — 18
Battle Museum — 44
Battle, St Mary's — 19
Bayham Abbey (EH) — 19
Beachy Head — 40
Bentley Wildfowl Centre — 41
Berwick, St Michael & All Angels — 19
Bewl Water — 41
Bexhill Museum — 44
Bexhill, St Peter — 19
Birling Gap — 41
Bishopstone, St Andrew — 20
Bluebell Line — 50
Bodiam (NT) — 12
Brede, St george's — 20
Brighton, Pavilion — 34
Brighton, St Peter, Preston Park — 20
Camber Castle (EH) — 12
Castle Hill, Seaford — 8
Charleston, Farmhouse — 35
Clayton, Jack and Jill Windmills — 52
Clayton, The Chattri Monument — 52
Crowborough, Conan Doyle Statue — 52
Cuckmere Haven/ Seven Sisters — 41
Cuckoo Trail — 54
Devil's Dyke — 8
Ditchling, Beacon — 8
Ditchling Museum — 44
Ditchling, St Margaret — 21
Eastbourne, Museum of Shops — 45
Eastbourne, Redoubt Fortress — 44
Eastbourne, RNLI Museum — 45
Etchingham, The Assumption & St Nicholas — 21
Firle Place — 35
Fletching, St Andrew & St Mary the Virgin — 21
Glynde Place — 35
Great Dixter House — 36
Hastings, 1066 Country Walk — 54
Hastings Castle — 13
Hastings, Shipwreck Heritage Centre — 45
Hastings, Smugglers Adventure — 45
Hastings, White Rock — 46
Heron's Ghyll, St John the Evangelist — 22
Herstmonceux, All Saints — 22
Herstmonceux Castle — 13
Herstmonceux, Science Centre — 46
High Rocks — 8
Horsted Keynes, St Giles — 22
Hove, British Engineerium — 46

Isfield, Lavender Line — 50
Jevington, St Andrew — 23
Kent & East Sussex Line — 50
Lavender Line — 50
Lewes, Anne of Cleves House — 46
Lewes, Barbican Museum — 47
Lewes Castle — 13
Lewes, Malling Down Nature Reserve — 41
Lewes, Priory — 23
Lewes, St Anne — 23
Lewes, St Pancras — 23
Lindfield, All Saints — 24
Lullington Church — 24
Lullington Heath National Nature Reserve — 42
Mayfield, Old Palace Chapel — 25
Mayfield, St Dunstan — 24
Michelham Priory — 25
Mountfield, All Saints — 25
Newhaven Fort — 14
Northiam, Great Dixter — 36
Northiam, Kent & East — 50
Sussex Line — 50
Pett Pools Nature Reserve — 42
Pevensey (EH) — 14
Piddinghoe, St John's Church — 26
Plumpton, St Michael & All Angels — 26
Pooh Corner (Hartfield) — 52
Rodmell, Monk's House (NT) — 36
Rotherfield, St Denys — 26
Rottingdean, The Grange Art Gallery & Museum — 47
Rye Harbour Nature Reserve — 42
Rye Heritage Centre — 47
Rye, Lamb House (NT) — 36
Rye, Museum — 47
Rye, St Anthony of Padua — 27
Rye, St Mary — 27
Rye, Ypres Tower — 15
Scotney Castle Garden — 36
Seaford, Martello Tower — 47
Sheffield Park (NT) — 36
Sheffield Park, Bluebell Line — 50
South Downs Way — 54
Southease Church — 27
Standen (NT) — 37
Sussex Border Path — 54
Ticehurst, Pashley Manor Gardens — 37
Vanguard Way — 54
Wadhurst, St Peter & St Paul — 27
Wakehurst Place (NT) — 37
Weald Way — 54
West Firle, St Peter — 28
Wilmington, Long Man — 8
Wilmington, St Mary & St Peter — 28
Winchelsea, St Thomas — 28
Winchelsea, Town Walls — 15

The **Sussex Wildlife Trust** is the leading conservation charity in Sussex concerned with the countryside and wildlife.

Our work includes:

- managing nature reserves
- helping people of all ages to enjoy wildlife
- advising landowners, communities, schools and individuals

You can call our **Conservation Careline** on **01273 494777** with your wildlife questions.

For information on membership, making a donation or helping as a volunteer please contact:

THE SUSSEX WILDLIFE TRUST
Woods Mill, Henfield, West Sussex, BN5 9SD. Tel: 01273 492630.
E-Mail: sussexwt@cix.compulink.co.uk Registered Charity No: 207005

CHESTNUT TREE HOUSE
CHILDREN'S HOSPICE

Over one hundred children in Worthing and the surrounding area have life-limiting illnesses. At present, these children and their families get little or no support. Parents rarely experience a break from 24 hour care of their sick child. Despite all the loving care received, most of these children will die before they reach adulthood.

Chestnut Tree House will provide specialised practical help, emotional care and support, and facilities to cater for the whole family, enabling them to share a better quality of life and enjoy their short time together. Support will continue for as long as it is needed after bereavement.

Over £3.5m is needed to build and to equip Chestnut Tree House, and another £1.5m to run it for the first year. The local community has shown great generosity and grants are also being sought from grant making trusts and companies.

For more information, or to make a donation, please write to:
Chestnut Tree House Appeal, St Barnabas Hospice, Columbia Drive, Worthing BN13 2QF, or telephone 01903 264147

Council for the Protection of Rural England

CPRE

CPRE works at national and local level to protect England's countryside by promoting good practice in conservation and discouraging unnecessary development.

CPRE Sussex branch works locally to protect the Sussex countryside from unsuitable development, promote improved services in rural areas and encourage good farming practices.

Sussex Branch

CPRE screens local planning applications and raises the alarm when necessary.

In Sussex **CPRE** supports the campaign for National Park status for the South Downs, and for improving facilities and development within local towns and villages to minimise further erosion of greenfield sites.

*If you share these aims and would like to support **CPRE** in Sussex, you can join the local branch. Annual membership can cost less than 40 pence a week - Individuals £17.50, Joint membership £23, Family membership £27.50.*

For details contact: CPRE Sussex Branch, Brownings Farm, Blackboys, Uckfield, East Sussex TN22 5HG. Tel. 01825-890975, email: CPREsussex@aol.com

Firefly Guide

West Sussex:

History · Culture · Landscape

ISBN 0951569112

£4.50 from all good bookshops, or post-free from Firefly Publications, Nima, Dappers Lane, Angmering, West Sussex BN16 4EN

Prehistoric Sites

Roman Remains

Castles

Cathedrals, Churches and Priories

Stately Homes and Gardens

Nature Reserves and Beauty Spots

Museums

Other Visits

Itchingfield - Priest's House

www.fireflypublications.co.uk